JOHN B. EDWARDS

The
BURDEN
of
COMMAND

A short primer on Supervision and the continuing efforts to
lead people and manage organizations in a modern context

2014

ISBN: 1495240444

ISBN-13: 9781495240447

ABOUT THE AUTHOR

John B. Edwards began his career in 1977 as a uniformed Deputy Sheriff at the Evans County Sheriff's Office. John joined the Georgia Bureau of Investigation in 1978, where he worked as an undercover agent, a narcotics and smuggling investigator, and in general investigations. In 1992, John was promoted to Assistant Special Agent in Charge and designed, staffed, and supervised the Tri-Circuit Multi-Jurisdictional Drug Task Force. John returned to the Statesboro Regional Field Office as the Assistant Special Agent in Charge in 1996. In 2000, John was appointed acting Special Agent in Charge of the Savannah Regional Drug Enforcement Office until 2001 when he returned to the Statesboro Regional Field Office as the Special Agent in Charge. In June of 2004, John served with F.B.I. and Secret Service as Co-Chair of Crisis Management during the Sea Island G-8 Summit. John retired from the GBI in October of 2008.

John was appointed Chief Deputy Sheriff in Evans County, Georgia in 2009 where he designed and implemented an Intelligence Led Policing Operation for the Evans County Sheriff's office. During this time Evans County was one of thirty agencies in the nation that was part of the Bureau of Justice Assistance's "Smart Policing Initiative" and Evans County was recognized as one of the ten best practices in the nation. In 2013, John became an executive board member and manager of the peace officers association of Georgia, the state's oldest and largest law enforcement association that promotes officers professional growth and development.

John has and continues to teach many investigative, intelligence, and leadership courses from originally designed curriculum throughout the country. John has lectured for The National Law Enforcement Institute in Santa Rosa, California, Counter Drug Academy, in Meridian, Mississippi, the International Association of Chiefs of Police, National Sheriff's Association, Department of Homeland Security, Bureau of Justice Assistance, F.B.I. National Academy Associates and various Federal, State and local Agencies.

John served as an adjunct instructor, teaching his personally designed course, "The Burden of Command," at the Georgia Law Enforcement Command College at Columbus State University. John consults for both national and international police agencies and has published numerous articles regarding the management of criminal investigations, major incident management, and law enforcement operations. He currently conducts three-day seminars throughout the country centering on "The Burden of Command" philosophy.

He co-authored his first book, "Successful Strategies in Criminal Investigations: Recognized Leaders in Law Enforcement on Responding to Community Needs, Utilizing New Technology, and developing Investigative Plans," in 2009.

John currently lives in Evans County, Georgia with his wife of 30 years, Anita, and his sons, J.B. and Mac.

PREFACE

This book represents the journey through the complexities of the human condition, and is a tool chest designed for and stocked to provide important, meaningful, and useful resources when given to leaders charged with the responsibility of management in today's workplace.

Unfortunately, many of us are promoted and thrown into the role of manager without the benefit of any training whatsoever. Thus, we subject our employees to trial and error supervision, and the job site becomes more of a research adventure than a functional mechanism for efficiency and effectiveness in expected job performance.

Often, we assume if a person is a great worker we can promote them and they will be great managers and continue to exceed our expectations. Leadership is the catalyst that brings forth the necessary influences and resources demanded by management. Work ethic, structure, and self-discipline sustain the management process. Great leaders and managers are not born; great leaders and managers are created by their experience, passion for the job, and training. This book is written for those thrown into the arena as new supervisors; this book is a tool to provide knowledge, discernment, and understanding to those to seed growth and performance in employees through a new and paradigm shifting perspective.

It all starts with us, with how we see, with how we decide, and with how we act. To maintain a certain ongoing self-discipline to accomplish this process of objective assessment is an absolute daily burden that we must incessantly carry. Consequently, I have struggled to write this book in such a fashion to provide enough detailed information and specific examples to enable its reader the ability to practically apply the information in their daily work. My hope and prayer is this book will be of great benefit and continuing utility to the multitude of great leaders who work so hard to do so much.

Many years of work for or around great supervisors, good supervisors, mediocre supervisors, poor supervisors and tyrants, along with 20 years of mistakes, failures, and successes as a supervisor have forged the resolve and produced the information to write this book. My journey came at the cost and expense of many people who, by their hard work, taught me so much, they taught me lessons that have become so valuable in my life.

Early in my career, I had the privilege of working for Johnny J. McGlamery, my "Senior Agent" and supervisor at the Georgia Bureau of Investigation field office in Statesboro, Georgia. Johnny was a premier leader who influenced everyone in our office in a positive way; he lead us, mentored to us, backed us, developed us, and grew us to be the best we could be. He taught us that mediocrity and the status quo had no place at the table at the "Region Five" field office. Johnny assured that we were the best and everyone would know it. Johnny placed a high premium on fraternity, fellowship and trust.

Moreover, Johnny McGlamery was a leader of the purist sort, a person who by his very nature carried great influence and respect. We followed him and would die for him, not because we had to, but because we wanted to. We felt an absolute loyalty for him and would become almost sick when we felt we did not meet his expectations. We knew he cared for us, that he cared for our work, our abilities, our problems and our attitudes. We knew that he trusted us and would stand up for us to the absolute end. We knew this because he modeled his behaviors with what he said; he walked the walk exactly like how he talked the talk. He always demonstrated a passion for our purpose, our mission and our work. Johnny McGlamery was "the real deal" and everyone knew it.

What I neither knew, nor understood until I became a supervisor, was how difficult Johnny's management style was to emulate. I had to fight against my own ambition and selfishness to manage like him. I had to hide my emotions and control my tongue to manage like him. I had to listen, be patient, stay calm, and be conscientious toward my own diverse and individual employees, who all were different, had their own strengths and weaknesses, and theory of the universe, to manage like him. I had to gain the courage to stand up for people and to correct people in positive and meaningful ways. I had to demonstrate the fortitude to put others first and work every day to grow and sustain my competence as the leader.

Harry Coursey, another supervisor I worked under, was totally different from Johnny in much of his philosophy. He was much more "specific-mission" focused and demanded timely results. However divergent their overall philosophies, they held much in common when it came to looking after and backing their people. Harry Coursey was determined to always prevail in any situation and Harry would do whatever he needed to do when dealing with substandard performance; Harry taught me the importance of holding people accountable for mission, organization, and service to stakeholders. If you worked and did your job, you grew and developed. And if you didn't, he dealt with you quickly and effectively. One could either step up or step down.

My longtime supervisor, upper management commander, friend and mentor Roy Harris impressed me early on by the value he put upon service, mission, performance and results. Roy passionately believed in the importance of an exemplary work ethic, passion for the job, competence in your craft and modeling all of those qualities for those under his command. His fortitude and courage were remarkable. Roy taught me the importance of love for my job and the requirement to never rise to any rank or level where you thought you did not have to work just as hard as you had always worked. His saying was the "agents would run at the speed of their boss."

My friend, mentor, and last Supervisor, Charles Sikes, taught me the values of servant-hood and unselfishness. Charles demonstrated how and why humble men often evolved and still do evolve into strong leaders. Charles had a constant and ongoing saying that he lived by, "horses and troops eat before the officers."

Charles taught me the value of being "unimportant" and holding others as "more important." His was very much a selfless philosophy, a philosophy that influenced and transformed my character to one that understood, understands, and embraces the great benefits of humility and servant-hood. Moreover, he taught me it was the right and the only way to be.

I first truly understood these lessons shortly after my promotion to Assistant Special Agent in Charge and the commander of the Tri-Circuit Multi-Jurisdictional Drug Task Force. To command like Johnny, Harry, Roy, and Charles did was daunting, more difficult than I had imagined; finally, I understood why bad supervisors were bad.

I learned that when one is placed into a position of command he must strive against and fight himself every day. You see, supervision and management are not natural human abilities. The leader must fight every day to maintain the requirements of those under his charge, as well as manage himself to be a mentor, servant, a great communicator, "the boss," and the only person in the group that is absolutely and totally responsible for everything. I quickly discovered that it is "A Burden to Command;" it is something that never ends or lets up.

The burden begins with knowing who you are, your weaknesses, your strengths, your pet peeves and your passions. Only after recognizing and managing these things every day can the leader work to not adversely impact those under him. This also incorporates the need of the leader to not undermine his interpretations.

I learned how important empathy toward others was in the work place, of being heard, of being understood. I learned not only did I have to successfully evaluate myself and then control my frailties, but that I had to listen, observe, and accurately interpret others with calculated empathy. Identifying their strengths and weaknesses, alongside particular niches and peculiarities, and then managing those within relationships to build trust and mutual respect became a large part of what I did.

This formula led to investments of relational currency that I deposited in the personal account of many employees, currency to use later in difficult and very human times when I had to do those things that required extra work, behavioral changes, or disciplinary action of my employees. Moreover, these investments were, by design, for them and they knew it, respected it, appreciated it, and became conditioned to expect it.

I learned the importance of putting others first, to take my job, purpose, and mission seriously and not myself. I discovered the more I did for others to make them better than me the more it came back for me. Once an employee sees their leader is all about them, they trust, take ownership, make decisions, and mimic their leader. What is important to their leader then becomes important to them.

I found how important it was for me to spend copious amounts of time studying, researching, and building my competencies in our craft in order to properly mentor and grow my staff's competencies. I learned how difficult it is to communicate, listen, gather credible and meaningful feedback, and, most importantly, learn. I learned early on that there are two sides to the desk: the subordinate's and the manager's. It is important to remember that, while you do need to seek and be aware of everyone's opinions, management is never an absolute democracy; the commander has the ultimate responsibility, one that sometimes requires the ultimate decision making.

Everyone expected me to listen, be fair, and then make decisions and deal with those that needed to be dealt with and reward those who did their jobs. The work environment, performance, and reputation depended upon the leader's ability to lead and the manager's ability to manage. Bottom line: I learned that if a problem developed in the work unit, the first place you better look is at yourself.

The combinations of experience and study from great works by great authors have also played a major role in this book's development. When I became a supervisor in 1992, it did not take me long to understand I would have to work and study to be a supervisor through not only first-hand experience and anecdotal research, but also academic research. The more I read, researched, discussed, and resolved to educate myself the more important the philosophy would be to me.

Works from Ken Blanchard, (One Minute Manager), Paul Hersey (Situational Leadership), John Maxwell, (many fabulous works on his role in leadership) and Peter Drucker's premier description of the workings of proper management influenced my development. Then came the research and work of Daniel Goleman regarding emotional leadership and then it all came together. I could relate and understand why the things that went right went right and why what worked did work. I began to understand where I had failed and where I had succeeded.

Goleman taught me about how emotions played such a huge role in my personal life and in those I supervised. Blanchard taught me the importance of letting people work; Hershey taught me how to work different people, and Maxwell brought it all together. Drucker gave context and meaning to what I was responsible for in my own supervisions and our relation to purpose and mission.

Finally, I have taught many classes at the Command College at Columbus State University on this subject and have given seminars across the country on this subject. All in attendance have asked for more so they may share my reflections, my "war stories," and my philosophy on the required influences and persuasion skills by leaders and the exemplary performance of functions and processes demanded by management. They all need to know how much more they have taught me from the many hours of interaction, stories, and real life experiences shared by these students, who were supervisors and managers from hundreds of different agencies and organizations. They too shaped this book.

I know what is within these pages and can assure with the greatest resolve, it works!

TABLE OF CONTENTS

INTRODUCTION

Merriam Webster defines "Command" as: *To exercise a dominating influence over (to have authority and command of)* **"Burden" as:** *Something that is carried (duty or responsibility)*

Command is a state where one is placed in a role of authority with a responsibility and requirement to lead others toward a common goal. A burden is something carried, in this case duty and responsibility, which is relentless and everlasting; difficulty comes when attempting to rest while carrying it. Moreover, with the responsibility of command comes burden; one cannot exist without the other. Thus, it is an absolute burden for one to take and sustain command. This burden occurs because we are humans commanding humans in a chaotic world that is constantly changing. As people, we find ourselves trapped in "the human condition," lost in our own being of ego, pride, ambition, selfishness, vanity, and lust. Self-centered, subjective, and belief-dominated through our entrenched individual culture and mindsets, the burden of command is the responsibility to overcome these adverse mindsets.

The story never changes and history repeats itself time and time again; when we factor in the human condition, we invariably tilt the equation toward conflict. The book of Genesis describes our true situation in detail and evolution teaches us the consequences in all life, that it is not the strong that survive, not the most intelligent, but those that adapt are the ones that survive.

Leadership and management are unnatural acts that require unnatural devotion and dedication to self-discipline in order to fight the nature of the human condition. That is why it is a constant and ongoing burden to command. The notion of putting others before self and releasing your authority to those others goes against the normative view of business and life.

Emotions are an integral part of what we are and who we are, they play huge roles in what we believe and how we shape the course of our behavior and conduct. Emotions can determine our attitudes and display our thoughts. We decide, assess, judge, and evaluate from emotions; we buy, sell, and bargain by emotions; we forge and cultivate relationships from emotions. We love, hate, enjoy, suffer; we are happy or sad; our emotions often govern us and everyone around us, help us relate and interact with the everyday. Emotions drive our very being and existence.

Based upon our dependency to and from our emotional human state and how such a dependency can dominate our behavior and those around us, would the ability to see ourselves from the outside looking in be valuable? Would our ability to shape and control our emotions with skill and to prepare for events and issues, rather than repair ourselves after such events or issues be of benefit? Would the ability to see others through their emotional interpretations in time to mitigate problems they encounter with us be of utility in our role as a manager? Would the promotion of good relationships as a result of this emotional intelligence lead to deposits of emotional currency in our subordinate's relational account and create a savings we can draw and borrow from later that would insulate us when times are bad for all involved? The answer is absolutely yes; when we know and understand who we are and how we are, then we can control how we think, talk, and act. That in and of itself is huge, now, if we observe and learn from our subordinates, and manage them through an "emotionally smart" context, it is only logical that we can produce benefits for them and, most importantly, mitigate problems.

What if we developed and sustained the highest level of competency within ourselves and, as a result, those under our charge developed, grew, and recognized that we were surely the best in our craft? What if they listened and learned from their "boss" and inherited that same level of competency in their own use for their current duties, future responsibilities and achievement of their goals and objectives in life? Would this be of benefit? That answer is yes.

What if your top priority was to develop and grow those under your command and you always took responsibility, never cast blame, always gave credit, and never took credit while always being honest, optimistic and purposeful? Would that have an effect on those under your charge? The answer is again, absolutely yes. Subordinates wouldn't worry about being thrown under the bus, and they would be trying to jump in front of it for you.

What if you became a skilled and great communicator who could understand and be understood, could cast vision and paint pictures of reality for those under your charge, ones through which they could fully understand every expectation and imagine every benefit? Would this be of importance and of continuing utility?

Finally, if you managed people in an open and fair way, held everyone to the same standards, the same performance measures, where good work was praised and rewarded, where poor performance was never ignored yet always corrected, where strong "mission-sense" and purpose blended with delegation to and ownership by subordinates, would the staff be efficient and effective? Again, absolutely and positively beyond any doubt, yes!

However, here is the problem: none of this can happen unless you make it happen. And to make it happen you have to sustain what it takes to make it happen. It is the "burden to command."

The human condition that we inherit and live with must be habituated and disciplined by us every second of every minute of every day to maintain the standards people expect to see in us and by us. The trick is this: we expect far more than we model and others are never judged in the same context as we judge ourselves. Therefore, we must be sensitive to the fact that we all expect far more ourselves and others than any of us can ever deliver.

These expected standards are the key elements in portraying and modeling our "burden of command" to others. And consequently, these standards work to achieve an inherit reputation for respect and credibility in leadership. They are fundamental and elementary core principles to not only command by, but to also live by.

But what are these standards, these cornerstones, which construct credible relationships that weave into the very fabric of our leadership mentalities? Purpose, responsibility, sincere care, and desire; all of these are the essential building blocks.

First, purpose is the drive that causes people to embrace a notion or idea as assign value. This process of adoption of purpose brings forth a mindset of pure devotion and dedication toward a particular ends, and to reach the requirements called for by that purpose, both defined and interpreted. Purpose starts as a spark that ignites a fire that burns deep within one's soul that, in turn, produces desire and persistence in all things. Once one is devoted toward a clear purpose and adopts its cause, takes ownership of that cause, then many skills, talents, and gifts are brought forth in order to create the circumstances to fulfill the requirements set forth to perform the best possible in pursuit of the goals and objectives associated with and by that purpose.

Purpose creates momentum, creates strength, creates condition; all of these things cause human beings to gain passion and drive for achievement, for success in any given responsibility, all in concert with that original purpose.

The commander must capture, identify, define, articulate, and incorporate purpose in all things. The central component in the casting of one's vision as a leader must contain a valid and worthy purpose that those under the leader's charge can and will buy into, something that gains their loyalty. Nothing in this life is more important than purpose; it trumps money, luxury, comfort, and selflessness. Purpose is the fuel for the fire of desire in the engine of the human condition.

With purpose comes the standard of and for responsibility, that lonely condition where your self-discipline requires you to do what you don't want to have to do. This is the very limit of liberty and freedom for the commander. John Maxwell frames it so well: "As you rise up in an organization you gain responsibilities and lose your rights." Commanders inherit positions of responsibility that require them to be responsible and accountable at all times.

Second, responsibility is easy to describe, but difficult to sustain in the realm of leadership. Taking responsibility means standing up when others run; it means taking the blame when others make excuses. Responsibility is a chore and must become habit; when one steps up to the plate, he must deliver what is expected or admit why he failed. Moreover, responsibility is oftentimes about fixing what's wrong to make everything right. Ego, feelings, and temperament have no place at the table of responsibility, but simply the combination of ethics, logic, drive, and desire to do the right thing at the right time for the right set of reasons.

Responsibility is clothed in trustworthiness and reliability by those who have seen it demonstrated, thus affecting all who benefit from its efficacy. The key resides in the proactive empathy demonstrated by one for the desire to provide practical and timely communication, communications that give meaning to and create insulation in today's information saturated environment. In other words, give those around you the information they deserve so they might make informed decisions and possess sound positions.

The way we frame and describe others in any relationship creates the mindset that set the stage for how we will receive, process, and prioritize information in our decision making. Ultimately, it will determine how we treat others. If we perceive someone as "stupid" or "ignorant," then that's how we will treat them; if we see through the lens of superiority, our behavior will follow suit. Thus, we do not treat people as equals but inferiors.

This is why we must be resolved to be devoted toward and loyal to the below four steps of dedicated behaviors designed toward giving others the respectful treatment required and deserved.

Step one: one's objectivity through humility; an open mind is central to the ability to judge others based upon what they are versus what you think. Once others are seen as worthy and valuable, then they are treated as such. Step two: one's ability to understand that everyone has an absolute right to information, input, and role in mechanical and societal actions, events, and issues during any relationship that affects them. Step three: one's ability to anticipate the consequences involved in and around the dynamic of those particular relationships. Step four: one's response as a result of those relationships.

Each response will be judged and evaluated by those in each particular relationship based upon content, context, and sincere dedication demonstrated by the reasonable leader responsible.

Reasonable leaders develop credibility and build reputations that become cornerstones to the construction of tremendously efficient and effective relationships. Commanders, as reasonable leaders, must constantly work to remain responsible to others; this labor requires devotion and dedication to hold one's self to the highest levels of concern, care, and responsiveness to and of others.

Responsible commanders inherit a desire to insure they cultivate subordinates into their adequate visions of leadership and performance purveyors. They realize such growth will transform every environment into a favorable one, one in which passions provide much better odds for the proactive solving of problems and set the best possible courses for success. Exemplary management, premier communication, and stellar leadership influence are deeply rooted in one's reputation for and to one's responsibilities.

Care is not and cannot be itself without sincerity; sincerity cannot be faked or disguised but must be a product of authentic and genuine concern based in respect, compassion, and conscientious concerns for others. Care is a standard people expect, one that builds trust and ultimately leads to the all-important ability to create and sustain relationships. Relationships are the most important phenomena in human existence and are central to any commander or leader.

Care is an expected result from people by other people; the condition it creates is fertile ground for the planting of relational seeds that grow into oaks that then grow strong into the most contrary winds of life. In life, adversity builds strength. When one has empathy with and to others, and factors in sincere care, relational currency is minted. This relational currency is key to investing in people, in setting up favorable situations, and creating an environment through which to receive big dividends toward the purpose and mission of the organization and influence of the leader. Trust is not given; it is not free, but earned. Such care is the first component of trust.

Desire is the necessity required in seizing the initiative in any given set of circumstances; desire causes one to gain interest, evaluate, and act. Excellent performance creates direct results in one's desire to do a job well. People with true desire contain burning passion to be the absolute best at what they do; they will not settle for second place.

Mediocrity is the partner of incompetence and failure, the despised enemy of the commander's designs, vision, and work. Desire is based upon one's divergence from mediocrity and his adherence to a state of mind through which he is in love with his work and burns with purpose for that work. Desire overcomes barriers, drives persistence, fuels optimism, and motivates the devotion to hard work.

Difficult circumstances and adverse conditions cannot defeat desire. Desire, when modeled correctly, is infectious, contagious to all who receive an ownership in its cause. Commanders that can consistently articulate purpose, demonstrate responsibility, communicate and perform care, and sustain premier motivation through desire, will become successful managers and great leaders.

Nonetheless, the greatest impediment to these four necessities is self, that human condition that perverts the inner good into an outer evil, one caring only for those primal desires, for pride, greed, envy, lust and selfishness. This culture of human selflessness works toward the famous "me" mentality in life. This adverse mindset creates the insecurity and paranoia-ridden thoughts that confer trauma upon many lives in the work place. Thus, one must harbor their personal passions and behaviors, fight toward self-awareness, self-management patience, and then obtain both social understanding and a working awareness of relationship management. Such will create environments where leaders can establish accounts within their subordinates where emotional currency can be deposited and spent in order to effectively and efficiently lead and manage.

It is a Burden to Command. Leaders must work to be trailblazers, and managers must lead to be forerunners. I have identified the five key "Burdens" one needs to carry upon himself if he is to achieve his goal, to sustain exemplary leadership skills, and acquire outstanding management results.

This book consists of five chapters, each describing a specific burden that the commander must bear and manage daily in order to be successful; they are as follows:

1.) **The Burden of Self-awareness:** Before we can influence others we must know ourselves; how do we act? How are perceived by others? How do we impact others? We must understand our moods, biases, and dispositions. We must understand our cultural and environmental influences. How do our sentiments affect the way others and how perceive them?

The leader must follow the example given in Goleman, Boyatzis and Mckees' outstanding book, "Primal Leadership." The leader must first recognize his problems and/or demeanors, dispositions, and behaviors, then work to manage those behaviors and conduct himself in such fashion that it does not adversely affect those under his charge. Then the leader must watch, listen, and become aware of the conduct of others, alongside their behavior, and probe and inquire when a sense of change and/or dissonance is perceived. The leader must possess the people skills requisite to develop relationships that led to candid and forthright dialogue and discussions. Moreover, the leader must look for ways to proactively develop emotional currency that can be deposited in their subordinates' emotional accounts. These deposits build for the leader to spend later on difficult issues.

2.) **The Burden of Competence:** A leader must be a mentor and teacher; how can your subordinates grow if you can't teach them the requirements of the craft? A huge stressor for employees lies in the incompetence of their supervisor. Poor decision making impacts the organization and every one in it. Leaders must know their "stuff" and be able to deliver at all times. Leaders must lead by example, and if they lack the knowledge and ability to make decisions or determine courses within the contexts of the situation afoot, they will lose "credibility" from all they supervise. The most important necessity for the leader is knowledge, then skill, and then development of craft. This process is perpetual and ongoing and must never ever stop. A competent leader is forgiven quicker because even if a competent leader lacks people skills in certain situations, his competence enhances those around them in an always-affirmative manner.

3.) **The Burden of Servant-hood:** Can you, as a leader, put the interests of others before yours? Can you sacrifice for others at a cost to you? The servant leader gains respect and favor from those around him when it is clear that the chief issues put forward are

"Purpose" and "People." The servant leader puts himself upon the altar of difficulty and labor to invest in building his people, cultivating his people with the overarching philosophy of "better." When subordinates see that a leader sacrifices on their behalf, such evolves into the greatest motivator.

4.) **The Burden of Communication:** One's ability to lead effectively is determined by his skills as a communicator. The value of communications among managers, supervisors, peers, and subordinates is tremendously important in all organizations. The efficiency and effectiveness of leaders within an organization rests upon dedication toward communication and cultivating skills that do so. Efforts to communicate must be deliberate and ongoing, working around and through barriers and different medians. 21st century technologies may enhance the manner through which we communicate, but, conversely, may adversely impact the way we communicate. An example: emails. While email is quick and real time, it often robs the parties of their observations of the so-important "non-verbal's" of those participating in such communications. This means that a message by email takes away the opportunity to observe the "unsaid"

Leaders must insure that roles and responsibilities drive and tailor communication routes and times versus relationships. Exemplary communications enhances leadership and provide stellar management.

5.) **The Burden of Management:** Leaders can never walk past poor performance, correct in private, or praise in public. Leadership is influence and management is process; people make processes work through the structured methods and manners directed by management. People must be rewarded when appropriate and held accountable toward their responsibilities and roles when appropriate. The important feature is how a leader insures the job is done, in the manner required by management, by those responsible for the work. The way a leader motivates, casts vision, and provides purpose is very important for the effectiveness and efficiency of the organization. Realistic goals and objectives in concert with "Ownership" displayed by subordinates in achieving those ends are central to success. Specific expectations, with freedom and input practiced by subordinates, and oversight and mentorship by leaders, is a recipe for absolute excellence. Management is a difficult and very unnatural behavior for human beings, especially when selflessness and ego create barriers toward the team's progress and performance. Such barriers create the paradoxical condition that often dooms a manager to failure. Only those managers that possess the knowledge, skills, and abilities to labor, evolve, and fight themselves every day to manage in the proper manner, at the proper time, in the proper place will become credible leaders and develop a reputation that is coveted by others.

This book is designed with the intent to integrate each chapter, or "burden," into each other for the purpose of demonstrating how one continuously interacts and affects the other. Each burden must be examined and studied not only in its totality, but also in unison with the others. This wholelistic review and continuous blend results in some repetitiveness. I ask that you forgive me and understand my intent. I believe it is necessary to my design to provide a product that mirrors my lectures and interweaves the information into the fabric of a continuing resource utility blanket or a body of management strategy and leadership behaviors. Also, please do not forget to use the epilogue as a means to tie my writings, the stories presented, and the research of many far more educated that I together.

Chapter One:

"THE BURDEN OF SELF-AWARENESS"

"If you have a problem with your office, work unit, or team…
the first place you better look is at yourself."

To know one's self is a gift and blessing, for once one knows and understands his weaknesses and shortcomings, strengths and advantages, and, as a result, trains himself for objectivity rooted in humility, combined with self-discipline, then he may manage himself.

I had to learn this the hard way when I was promoted to my first command. I quickly absorbed that everything changed when I crossed the bridge from one side of the desk to the other. Going from being responsible for "me" to being responsible for a group was and is a huge leap in one's life. To make things significantly more difficult, I did not have the benefit of any training; I had to learn to be a manager on the go. The age-old method of trial and error quickly took effect. I joined the countless others that had been cast into the position of "work-without-blueprints." So what does one do but innovate and look for help? For me, the key was fashioned from those on whom I could drop my ego, on whom I could call for help, advice, guidance and council.

I went to my friends in management positions and to books about leadership and management; through conversation and reading, I learned every day. The most humbling learning experiences came from those under my charge. My subordinates taught me much very quickly, and I remember taking back every critical word about my former bosses.

The agency, department, division, or work unit always reflects its leadership. The boss sets the stage and the pace for everyone. That is why one's conduct, behavior, work ethic, and communications acumen are so vital to the process. What one preaches, what one models, what one is, and what one does forges the "culture" of his work place and those who fill the positions under his charge. One's decisiveness, eagerness, optimism, and performance affect everything around him. One's ability to effectively listen, communicate, and interact is critical to moving forward in all endeavors. One's ability to know himself, as well as those around him, plays a huge role in the relational formula that achieves optimum performance and people's devotion, dedication, and loyalty. One must have empathy for others while maintaining fairness and motivation; keep the work place "in sync" to achieve best results.

Central to one's success as a manager, work as a leader, and responsibility as a Commander resides in his Emotional Intelligence, or his EI skills. In 1992, when I was appointed as the Commander of the Tri-Circuit Drug Task Force, I knew I had better get started improving my managerial skills and ascertain what I could regarding the requirements of leadership. I had been in leadership positions throughout my career, but one never so structured in an ongoing status.

When I first read about the concept of EI in "Primal Leadership" by Daniel Goleman, Richard E. Boyatzis, and Annie McKee, I was intrigued by both its controversial and paradoxical title and subject matter. How could one combine emotionally heartfelt, and by its very nature subjective driven, understanding with intelligence, rationale, and logically objective based understanding? After my study of the subject, it was clear that the whole notion about emotional intelligence boiled down a simple, basic, and fundamental behavior that promoted empathy, understanding, and positive influence.

It all begins with a leader's self-awareness – a recognition feature. The importance of the leader to possessing emotional self-awareness as it relates to their moods, feelings and actions, is paramount. Keen and accurate interpretation of self-awareness is a precise and useful self-assessment of one's actions and conditions. Following behind these is the all-important condition of self-confidence, a process where one demonstrates through his communications and demeanors that he is in fact comfortable in the shoes he wears at any given time.

Next is the leader's self-management – a regulation feature. Here the leader must demonstrate self-control, trustworthiness, conscientiousness, adaptability, achievement-drive, and initiative. The above two components, self-awareness and self-management, deal with the leader and his struggle to recognize and manage conduct and behaviors that are specific to his experience. The next tier deals with those he leads and manages. Social awareness – a recognition feature – deals with being empathetic, service oriented, and organizationally aware with those under one's command. Relational management – a regulation feature – deals with developing influence upon others, exemplary communication, model conflict management, excellent leadership, consummate change management, outstanding teamwork and collaboration, and an adept prowess at relationship cultivation.

These structures of self-awareness and self-management for leaders, paired with social awareness and social management of subordinates, are critical to the successful management and effective leadership today's workplace requires. When I read this recipe for leadership, I knew it proved what I had learned and knew all along. Moreover, it illustrated to me what I had seen perpetuated over the years by those supervisors who were so effective and efficient, yet so respected and honored.

John Maxwell, in his "Five Levels of Leadership," describes such leaders as those who have reached the pinnacle of Level Five, the zenith of "personhood." But what is "personhood?" Simply, the term "personhood" refers to the act of subordinates following a leader based on that leader's representation within an organization and, more importantly, what the leader stand for within and organization. To achieve the requirements of self-awareness is easier said than done; it is extremely difficult for us to see ourselves objectively and to assess our daily behaviors through the lens of others. Such is why the ability to build relationships that encourage accurate and truthful feedback from subordinates and one's peers is so vital. Feedback allows a leader to continually attain a state of self-awareness, thus enhancing his ability to remain responsible. Only when we have an accurate reflection of our self-awareness can we properly and successfully deal with our self-management.

The same also applies to our ability to remain socially aware of others; we must build an environment and sustain a culture of trust and effectiveness to promote openness and conversational democracy.

I will be honest: I cannot sing well. However, and often to my detriment, I sometimes believe I can. Whether this is alcohol induced or a product of a morning's shower, I rouse my ego and position myself to step to the karaoke stage. Thank goodness I have a wife who speaks truthfully and tells me what I need to hear; as a result, she prevents me from embarrassing myself – and her, perhaps – and protects me from the vegetable throwers. If a leader has people like my wife who are frank and truthful based upon, and rooted in, what they truly believe, then that leader has developed a huge asset in the workplace.

Aggressive and empathetic listening can be a leader's greatest asset in remaining socially aware of work place surroundings. Further, these same skills become equally important in the social management arena. These skills build credibility and trust and mold the environment into a forge of sound relationships. Naturally, most people want to be important to the Commander - you; they want to be important to the organization and its purpose in the work place. They want to have a say in what leaders do and how leaders go about doing it; when a leader takes a proactive position in listening to subordinate feedback, and then incorporating portions of that feedback into the organization's leadership strategies, extremely positive results occur and performance is most certainly enhanced.

When managers create and sustain a culture that promotes harmony through their efforts to effectively manage themselves while managing others, positive things happen and credibility takes hold, thus allowing a sound reputation to develop and grow. These reputations set the stage for positive perceptions and predictable realities for those at work to savor. This forges a healthy and productive environment that can weather storms and produce good results in bad times. This also creates a work place that can adapt and handle change quite well under adverse conditions and the worst of unexpected circumstances. This attribute alone is priceless in 21st century management conditions. Moreover, this culture creates, promotes, and sustains positive relationships within the work place.

Relationship management is often incredibly difficult to maintain at the exact level one wishes. Relationships between management and workers are constantly evolving, and changes in the tangibles and intangibles of the human condition and workplace situations make prognostication difficult. Inherent relational tensions, in concert with critical and often fluctuating balances between subordinates' issues and an organization's mission, make management difficult to handle correctly every time. Thus, one must be deliberate and determined to use every available skill set to maneuver the territory and capture the advantages available.

These advantages can facilitate smooth transition through contrary forces in swiftly changing environments where leaders are consistently required to conduct evaluations and promote good decision-making processes. The value of relationship building and factual information within your organization becomes tremendously important aspect of this sensitive balance that leaders weigh.

The previous deposits of relational currency by the leader can be drawn upon to promote unwelcomed work without adverse issues projected toward the Commander. It comes down to this: the more one puts in, the more one may withdraw.

There is a mental and emotional affect upon the leader that comes with making any decision regarding a "personnel issue," issues that impact people's lives and their families lives in very delicate ways. When you hit someone's emotional being, they tend to lose the rational side of being, become unable to interpret information in an objective way. More often than not, they don't care about the analysis or rationale; all they can process is the result as it applies to them and them only. When they lose that availability to reason and remain logical because their pathos has dominated their entire mindset, then the leader works from a difficult position, one that sometimes may be impossible to change.

This is why it is so important to be prepared for the emotional affect hurtling toward you. This debt against one's status quo account affects his ability to maintain the homogeneity among his staff and ripples into residual effects, most adverse. One may second-guess himself and others, question fairness, objectivity, and utility in real decisions and affect his actions. The questions always become this: Why did he do it? How did he do it? Did he even need to do it, and did he have to do it?

This is why motive, intent, analysis, rationale, and process are so very important in the personnel decision matrix. More often than not, the issue will always track toward people's efforts to frame the problem as personal and/or political. The work histories, politics, and relationships of people will highlight any issue of work performance. The manner and method of any evaluations will be challenged. The usual claims of prejudice or bias, from whatever cause, may, in fact, manifest.

When one makes decisions and creates effects that impact and affect people's feelings, freedoms, livelihood, and finances he drives deep-rooted emotions into the relational pool. Be ready for responses, resistances, and results; they're coming. The methods and manners of preparation and factual basis to support conclusions are huge. One's motives, intent, analysis, rationale, and process will provide him the tools to mitigate, argue, or defend his position first, to himself, and then to others who have judged or will judge.

However, there are two factors to weigh when looking from the outside in. First, did you strive to promote objective fairness under the facts and circumstances? Second, was and is your process consistent and totality transparent? These are central components to a good ending with premier results. Remember that you have inherited a tremendous responsibility when you accept a position of authority within the organization as a leader. It is not just about you anymore; you are now responsible to and for many others. Your organization expects and your people deserve the best conditions and performance. You must make difficult decisions, often under very difficult circumstances at very difficult times, decisions that may adversely affect many people. That is your job and you must do your job right. You asked to go into the oven where the heat lives; you must develop the fortitude, courage, knowledge, and abilities to deal with it! Always factor in care, compassion, and legal and ethical processes clothed in humility and rooted in fairness before moving forward for the good of the order.

In my classes, I carry a clear plastic jar about the size of a coffee can alongside about 25 small, multi-colored rubber balls that, when put in the bin, fill it to the brim. I use these items to demonstrate how a leader might invest and build a relational inventory based upon the way he interacts and manages people under his supervision.

I tell stories. I hold up the empty jar and put a ball in the jar each time after I tell a story about something I did as a leader that positively impacted an employee of mine. After I had tell numerous stories of empathetic and positive impacts in support of those under my charge, the jar is full of balls.

Then, I tell stories of when I required subordinates to work more under adverse conditions and the times I had asked for them to step up to the plate, sacrifice, and give more than usually required them. Then I take balls out of the jar. This demonstrates how and why the creation, development, and growth of relational stock is so important when the tension and stress of management causes a leader to adversely impact his people. The more balls in the jar, the more balls were and are available to take.

Remember, from basic rhetoric studies, Socrates always argued to find the truth, while the sophist argued to put for the greatest skills of oratory to win. Always follow the example of Socrates to dig, examine, and peel away until you discover the evidence – if it exists – to find the truth of the matter. Then you and others around may sleep better at night.

One's self-awareness, self-management, social awareness, and relational management skills are huge and super important, but so is his reputation and respect in the organization from his superiors. When one handles his business and other people's business well, this in and of itself is a tremendous credibility builder for him and his superiors. When one doesn't make problems, his supervisors can spend their time more effectively on projects without the distraction and drudgery of fixing those or other problems. Thus, it is absolutely amazing the kudos and relational currency one might get for just doing his job. Guess what happens when one far exceeds his superior's expectation in his job responsibilities. I'll give you a clue: great performances equals great respect and great respect equals better treatment. A wise man would rather put his money on an ugly horse that he understands will win instead of a beautiful horse that trots in last.

Now, if one earns that reputation and sustains that work ethic and work performance, he becomes a very good investment for anyone whose heart rests in the success of the organization. The theory of ownership again: if it's mine and you make it better, I like you for what you have done for me. Is that not simple enough to understand?

So, if one can build this type of reputation, one that translates into credibility, trust, and loyalty, his Commanders will place him in a better position to obtain permission for opportunity, obtain additional resources, and hold favor in the eyes of management. However, the issue then becomes one of context; if one uses his newfound clout for himself, he's instantly a suck up or climber; however, if one only uses it for his people and their needs, he's branded a servant leader with a boon of political influence. The key is how one uses influence and if one spends it on others for the good and purpose of one's organization. Moreover, such acts put one in the unique position of power, a position to help one's own people develop and grow.

As noted above, central to one's position to be able to lead and manage in a more proficient manner is one's ability to garner respect and build political clout from those above him. When one "works" one's way into a position of respect based upon doing his job, being loyal to his organization, and being a "builder" not a "bitcher," a "can doer" and "will doer" versus a "don't want to doer" or "can't doer," things get easier.

I've found that to achieve this goal of respect from one's superiors, one must first take care of and exceed in three separate but equal phases of life: private life, public life, and professional life. One must be responsible and insure he does not create issues or cause problems that could be perceived poorly by the public, his employees, or his supervisors. The management of emotions, actions, and words are tremendously important features to use in daily life in.

"Stay above the red line" within your professional policies and procedures; always tailor your conduct and behavior for proactive advancement of the mission. Carefully craft your words and actions to be empathetic toward the other person's position and maintain the respect and situational awareness to never become involved in any conflicts of interest. Help people be the best they can be every chance you get. Never expose your management or exploit your superiors in a negative manner. Always factor in your responsibility to be objective, supportive, and a team player when it comes to the mission and purpose of your organization. Strive to become the "go to" person for your superiors, filled with competence, tempered in humility, motivated with attitude, controlled by optimism, and personified by passion for purpose driven accomplishment. Manage your way up and down the chain – and even sideways – with your peers to develop the positive reinforcement everyone needs and appreciates in the work place and around the organization.

In the GBI, headquarters would send an inspection team down from Atlanta to the field office to examine files, observe facilities, inventory vaulted evidence, evaluate performance, and interview employees and clients in the region regarding the management team. This happened every two years. The team would usually have a ranking inspector and two to three other supervisors from regional offices around the state; the team spent at least three days on site to accomplish their mission. The intent of this process was to promote uniformity in GBI operations, insure compliance with policy, and mitigate potential problems before they could occur. Any great command staff knows and believes in the old adage, "in order to expect you must inspect." So do proactive managers; Deputy Director Tom McGreevy, a former boss of mine in the late 70's, had a saying: "Supervision is 10 percent telling and 90 percent checking up on."

I had been through many inspections as an agent and supervisor, and I appreciated their willingness to learn and "show off" certain aspects of performance, of innovation that could then be toted back to Atlanta to the Director's, innovations that would grab his attention. Most of the time, in order to obtain that attention, one must either be in the midst of crisis or be part of a problem they are having to deal with. Because of this, I welcomed every opportunity allowed me to, in some capacity, command the "big boss's" attention on my own terms, in my own time; being in Inspection gave me those windows of opportunity and bits of time. I also learned how I could use the inspection process to manipulate my bosses and my staff in tandem, but manipulate them for very positive results. Central to this strategy: leave me out of everything and focus on them. This type of play evolved into a winning formula that promoted the health, security, and welfare of my office.

Here is what I did and how I did it:

When the inspection team arrived, the inspector would, first, always call a staff meeting to introduce the inspection team, elucidate on what they would be doing, and outline the importance of their mission process. I would keep quiet until the meeting was over, then I would ask the inspector for permission to speak, stand, look around the room to insure all my people were present, then stare the inspector in the eye and say*: "Inspector, whatever you find good in this office, these outstanding and hardworking agents and staff have accomplished… if you find anything bad, I and I alone am responsible."* This captured attention; this let everyone know that the responsibility rested with me. My people knew they would not be "thrown under the bus," and the inspection team knew there would be no excuses. It was always a win-win scenario.

Once the inspection team began their probe, I would always ask the inspector into my office for a "secret" meeting. Once I had captured his attention, I would go down the list of my staff and tell them what they would hear and learn from the inspection team's interviews of my staff in a few days. I was very specific and brought out the positive and the negative, always careful to be as accurate as I could in my forecast of issues, concerns, gripes, and general theory of the universe. The inspectors always were gracious to me, listened empathically, and some would even honor me – or perhaps humor me – by taking notes.

Then I would hand the Inspector a stack of 3x5 index cards; etched on each card was a staff member's name, a date, and a short, but very descriptive synopsis of something they had excelled in or an outstanding job they had most recently completed. I would then request the Inspector to promise me that during the course of our three-day inspection, they would approach my particular employee and recognize their outstanding work effort and performance, brag on them, and leave me out of everything.

They would follow my wishes on each of my people, and I knew, without seeing or hearing, the powerful position of respect it engendered in them for me. I cared and wanted them, not me, to get the credit. Further, it gave me cultivated greater credibility that I would never ever sacrifice them for my sake; they knew I would back them 1000 percent because I always put them before me. Always.

When the last day of the inspection came, the Inspector always sat down with the Agent in Charge to share the results of the employee/staff interviews, results regarding the organization, its management, and any other thing on a particular employee's mind. Inspectors would always say to me: "Well, what you told me the other day is exactly what they said during the interviews, so apparently there is nothing I can update you on or make you aware of…" I would thank the inspector and advise them of what strategies I would implement to fulfill their vision or mitigate any concerns.

I knew the value of creating culture within the workplace, one where one's staff was quick to tell him what he needed to hear, what he wanted to hear. To sustain this culture, I did a lot of listening; I encouraged participation in decision-making; I admitted when I was wrong, when I had made a mistake, or when I had failed to control my emotions. It was a very much more work, but seldom, if ever, do I remember being surprised because a staff member did not vent or complain to me first, trust me with his thoughts. A great example of this, of where observations, follow up, and feedback came into play, comes to mind, but under a new and different set of circumstances and descriptions.

It was when I ran the drug enforcement office in Savannah, Georgia.

I walked into my office one morning, waded through an in-basket that was stacked so high "a show dog couldn't jump over it;" there were boring file reviews everywhere. I needed caffeine to get through it all. So, while walking out of the kitchen holding my routine morning diet coke, I saw one of my agents walk past with his head down; he didn't say a word. This definitely wasn't normal, and, for me, it was "clue," a sign that something was wrong. Consequently, I followed up on my suspicions by walking into his office, sitting down with my diet coke, and simply taking the time to ask, "What's up."

Immediately, a red hue took over his light complexion, his hands started shaking, and in a cracking voice he said, "Boss… I'm going to be fired." Now, that got my attention quick; I straightened up in my chair and asked what in the world was wrong. He replied: "I've lied on a search warrant affidavit and have false information that has been before the judge." My heart really sunk; he was right. If he had lied under oath, he would be fired and, more importantly, most likely prosecuted for a crime, too. I straightened higher in my seat, got solid eye contact and said, "Tell me about this in specifics."

He said that he had put together an affidavit for a search warrant for a big dope dealer up the road in a nearby County, that he had provided the judge with the warrant, swore to its truth, and the judge signed the warrant. He advised that after the warrant had been signed, he got back to his car and saw where the warrant was wrong. The computer program that facilitates the construction of the document had duplicated a set of statements from a previous warrant that had nothing to do with the current case. Thus, in his mind, he had committed false swearing and produced an invalid warrant. He had been up all night, worried, depressed, and anxious over what to do. He knew he should have proofread the warrant to insure its accuracy and veracity, but he had not. And now he would suffer the consequences. He stated he didn't know what to do and had made up his mind to tell me that morning. However, he was glad I confronted him first.

I asked again to insure the warrant had not been served and got the facts to verify, in my mind, it was in fact a series of computer and editorial mistakes absent of any dishonest intent. Then I told the agent meet me at my car; we drove to meet the district attorney and explained the failure, then, with his understanding and blessing, we went to the judge that signed the warrant. We explained the situation to him, produced a mea culpa, brought forth a correct copy and ultimately remedied everything in an ethical, moral, and legal manner.

As we rode back to the office, the agent apologized again and again, thanked me again and again for saving him, and then brought up the big "disciplinary action" question. I asked him to tell me what he had done wrong, and he began a long description of his lapse in computer use blended with the failure to employ the age old safeguard of proofreading. I then asked him his plans to keep this from ever happing again. He replied with a long litany of preventive measures in combination with a greater sense of the importance of content and context of legal documents before they ever go before the judge. He ended by saying it would never ever happen again.

I told him I thought he had done a very detailed job of articulating his poor performance, defining the consequences of his poor performance, and formulating the plan to insure the poor performance never happened. Again, all I had to do was follow up to insure his plans worked and be there to support him. I often wondered what would have happen if I had not recognized the "blimp on the radar" and probed the issue afoot. In management, the sooner one can identify a problem and move to deal with it, the better.

During my assignment as Commander of the drug task force, I was responsible for working in cooperation with one University police chief, one Georgia State Patrol Troop Commander, five Sheriffs representing five Counties, eight Chiefs of police from eight Municipalities, three District Attorneys – who represented the three judicial circuits that covered the jurisdictions of the chiefs and sheriffs – and the GBI regional office and drug office. A total of 20 members sat on my task force "control board" and provided operational and policy oversight.

We met every third Thursday to discuss operations, administration, and any issues afoot. I learned early on to always sustain outside contact and develop outside relationships everywhere I could. I would always work out issues before any meeting to mitigate surprises. Thus, the meetings always went smoothly, and unanimous votes among the members were commonplace. Relational and relatable cultivation, access and availability, and proactive and structured communication facilitated these smooth meetings.

Furthermore, I learned the value of going out of the way to find solutions to my stakeholder's problems. In order to achieve an advantage in this quest, one must work a little harder than usual. Below, I illustrate how one must sometimes work under difficult circumstances to find a better way to give that obligatory and difficult "yes" answer, as opposed to that continually easy "no" answer.

Most drug taskforces have two resources smaller agencies do not possess; first, undercover officers. Second, adequate funding for these officers to buy drugs from dealers while the officers operate in their covert roles or capacities. In rural areas, it is important for these undercover operations last several months, operations where the hidden identity of the officer allows the opportunity to buy off as many drug dealers as possible.

One afternoon, a Sheriff called me about a problem he had in his county. He told me citizens were talking badly about him, saying he was a "crook" because a store in the county sold beer on Sunday, and, consequently, this caused all kinds of problems with adult and under-age drinking. At this time, it was against state law to sell any type of alcohol on Sunday. The Sheriff said he had to have help, and he wanted me to use one of my undercover officers to buy beer from the store on Sunday and execute a search and seizure warrant to confiscate the beer thereafter.

Now, what I could have said, and been perfectly within my role of responsibilities, was this: "Sheriff, under our federal grant funding, the money we are given can only be used for drug enforcement. Moreover, if I use one of my officers to buy your beer and, as a result, you execute a search warrant and arrest the clerk, then we have exposed our officers' identity and destroyed his ability to work undercover in your county buying drugs from big time dopers. Further, drug distribution is a serious felony, while beer sales are a misdemeanor." Now, this Sheriff would most certainly not want to hear this and, in his mind, this situation was not a strategic crime issue, but a political and personal problem aimed toward the defamation of his character.

Instead, what I said was this: "Sheriff, you know how important it is to your citizens and to you that we are able to fight the drug problem in your county to the best of our ability. It is important to you, ethically, to complete your job responsibility and politically when people reflect back on that job responsibility. Now, if I send one of our officers over to buy beer and serve a warrant, we eliminate the opportunity to use that officer to work illegal drug sales in your county, and you lose the opportunity demonstrate your job responsibilities as a success in that effort. Now, what we can do is this: I will call my friend in Savannah at the drug squad, and see if we can't borrow one of their undercover agents; if you don't mind swearing them in as a deputy, furnishing their travel expense funds, alongside the requisite beer purchasing funds, then I'll cover the transaction, record it, document the buy, and write your affidavit for the search warrant based upon the undercover officers' buy. Then, you and your deputies can serve the warrant, arrest the clerk, and seize the beer."

The Sheriff was happy and complimented me with a litany of thanks. I made all the arrangements and the deal went like clockwork. He got his bust, respect from the citizens, and value from his task force because we looked toward helping him, not simply saying, "No." Now, do you think I got some mileage from this Sheriff on this issue and do you believe it earned me some relational currency? The answer is, yes, it absolutely did; he was a huge supporter of our squad and was the first to always try to help me.

It is more difficult to say the difficult "yes" versus the easy "no;" a lot depends upon the way we see things and what priority we give people. The true measure of a friend is when they help you despite having no guarantee of something in return. So much of our culture is based upon a "me" mentality, on what "I" can get out of something. Further, some people, when given authority, have no sense whatsoever what empathy does not factor into their equation. They are more concerned with pushing their agenda, of "taking and getting," instead of "sharing and giving."

When a person is given rank or put in a position over another, they often develop a "freedom" to dominate others and will either see the opportunity as a purpose to better others, themselves, and the organization or as an opportunity to run things the way they want it.

Then there are many who possess the true passion for people and organization, but do not understand how to translate that into proper behavior because they are prisoner to their selfish views, their selfish perceptions of those around them; they often do not stop to analyze themselves, their conduct, and how they are themselves perceived.

Experience has taught me that three types of personalities exist within all people, three personalities that domineer or influence their beliefs, attitudes, and behaviors.

These three personality types are:

1. Bullies, Haters, and Takers: these are self-serving, selfish tyrants that adversely impact others' lives and cause problem after problem within and outside the organization. They spoil opportunities, damage relationships, prevent trust, and destroy collaborations.

2. Watchers, Waiters, and Apathetics: these turn blind eyes to what is right and, as a result, defeat anyone's desire to take a stand, or to have a position on anything. They would simply rather not get involved or place themselves in any situation where they can't wriggle out from an issue or deny their responsibilities. They never want to be put in a position where they can be held accountable under adverse conditions.

3. Helpers, Lovers, and Givers: these look toward what they can do versus what they can't do, and strive to give rather than take. Their unselfish character denies self and puts others first. They have a genuine care and concern for people, value relationships, and promote harmony and purpose. Helpers and Lovers will take risks and self-sacrifice to insure others have opportunity and the capacity to enjoy success.

Often, one of these three becomes the dominant pattern that shapes the way we describe, see, and treat others. The manner in which we describe people will often match the way we treat them. If one degrades or devalues another, then he has fewer reservations on being ugly or hateful toward them. If one sees good and potential in another and recognizes his value and worth, then he will treat the other as important and see to the other's needs and wellbeing. Such illustrates why it is so very important that we strive every day to shape our mental outlook and fashion our inner feelings toward the latter of the three.

At one point or another, we all have been and will be influenced by these types of characteristics; we must insure we never fall into the consistent and easy pattern of the first two. It is a burden to first be self-aware of becoming victim to the temptation of the Bully and Watcher, but tremendously important we remember the value of the Helper, an archetype that will emphatically change our outlooks and behaviors for the ultimate better.

The ability and skill of a Commander to see theirs and others' emotions objectively – perceive the emotions, understand the emotions, manage the emotions and channel the emotions in a productive manner – is paramount in the endeavor of successful leadership in today's workplace.

Moods, impulses, optimisms, alongside self-confidence and self-regard, assertiveness, empathy, awareness, sincerity, flexibility, adaptability, stress-toleration, and problem-deduction are all so critically important in the workplace and in the leader's repertoire. The success or failure of a Commander to lead in an exemplary way depends upon the Commander's ongoing and constant quest to remain self-aware and his disciplinary ability to translate that awareness into positive and fruitful behavior and conduct.

One's feelings are the catalyst for his thoughts and his thoughts drive his decisions and behaviors. This is why the management of self and the management of emotion is vastly important to one's success as a Commander. The ability to understand and regulate and control one's emotions provides the optimum environment and atmosphere to synchronize, influence, and manage other's emotions. To paraphrase

James Carville, "It's their feelings, stupid." One must start with himself before he can begin with others.

In closing, The Harvard Business Review published an article in September 2008 titled, "Social Intelligence and the Biology of Leadership" by authors Daniel Goleman and Richard Boyatzis. When I read it, I knew immediately it would become a jewel in the leadership box. Their hypothesis was this: behavior can energize or deflate an entire organization through what they termed, "mood contagion." They put forth the notion that when one laughs often and sets an easygoing tone, he triggers similar behaviors from those around him. Further, they pointed out that bonded teams function better than fragmented teams. They link this "mood contagion" to neurobiology. Positive behaviors, such as demonstrating and exhibiting empathy, create a chemical connection between leader and follower. Goleman and Boyatzis proposed that increasing one's social intelligence, his skills, and his abilities, one could foster and enhance the neurobiological changes that create positive behaviors and emotions in his subordinates.

I can testify these social strengths have tremendously helped me navigate the dynamic landscape a Commander traverses in both good and bad times, and with good or bad issues afoot.

- Empathy: understanding what motivates other people, even those from different backgrounds; being sensitive to others needs.
- Attunement: listening attentively and thinking about what others feel; attuned to others moods.
- Organizational Awareness: appreciation of one's group, team, or organizational values and culture; understanding the social networks and knowledge of the unspoken norms.
- Influence: persuasion of others by engaging in discussions, appealing interests, and obtaining the support of key individuals.
- Development: coaching and mentoring others with care and compassion; personally investing time and energy in mentoring

and providing feedback that others find meaningful in their development and growth.

- Inspiration: articulating a compelling and purposeful vision; building team or group pride; fostering positive emotional tone and cultivating the best in each individual.
- Teamwork: encouraging the participation of everyone on one's team; support of all members; fostering cooperation

These seven areas are required for a Commander to have positive interaction, but they won't work if one can't see his personality issues, habits, characteristics, and weaknesses, all those things that may derail his efforts. The best intentions are meaningless if not applied properly. One must be objective, open-minded, self-aware, self-regulated, and self-managed.

Daniel Goleman once said during a Harvard lecture, one regarding emotional intelligence and social intelligence, "Get out and get some feedback." The ability to drop one's ego, embrace humility, and have the courage to solicit the views of others regarding how he performs and their interpretations of his behaviors and ideas, is tremendously important toward one's ability to sustain awareness in the workplace.

I remember in 1992, as a new supervisor, I asked an agent about my supervision of a particular operation. He replied that I had become "inconsistent" with my management in both the manner and method that I used in treating him equal to two other agents. As I listened to him, I got mad – I got heated even – and thought how, if he behaved like the others, he would not be so worried about it; he wouldn't be so sensitive.

Then, I stopped; I pushed those "superior-me" thoughts out of my mind and tried to adopt his angle of view, to give it ample weight. When I did, I found myself questioning the way I had behaved and saw things from his perspective, now enlightened.

In the final analysis, he might not have been totally right, and I was not totally wrong. But his perception and opinion had merits and, as a result, I was and am convinced I evolved into a better supervisor, became more consistent in my treatment of him, and gained his respect and loyalty because of my outreach to him, my attention, and my objective listening to his views.

One must look into the mirror as a Commander, to see and evaluate his own conduct first before he might look out the window to judge others; such is the requirement needed to build a credible structure upon which the totality of all facts and circumstances in any given scenario or situation might be placed. If one can see things clearly and completely, and then evaluate issues thoroughly and accurately, the chances for the best results multiply, and the possibilities of unintended consequences and adverse risk scenarios diminish.

Nothing is as valuable as a proactive mindset and culture in today's world. As John Maxwell said, "You can either prepare or repair." Central to preparation as a Commander is one's ability to remain aware of himself and others and those issues that result from relationships, issues, incidents, and events that create the landscape in his particular occupation or craft.

The autocratic means of management and the authoritarian style of leadership are analogous to the title of Margaret Mitchell's old novel, "Gone with the Wind." Today's employees, teams, and work place personnel will not tolerate or sustain that paradigm. The modern Commander, supervisor, manager, and/or "boss" is required understand that he must evolve into the democratic, practice the inclusive means of leadership that begin with the feelings, beliefs, and wants of others and morph into motivating those same individuals toward the organizational purposes and goals.

It all starts with what you as a leader value and believe; it all starts with your ability to objectively perceive, understand, and manage your own emotions.

It all begins with you.

Chapter Two:

"THE BURDEN OF COMPETENCE"

*"People tolerate struggling leaders when their level of competency is so high
that their subordinates grow and develop from them."*
*"Not many of you should become teachers, my brothers and sisters, for you
know that we who teach will be judged with greater strictness."*
James 3:1

Dr. Curtis McClung, a mentor of mine and of many others at Columbus
State University's Command College, once told me: "Wisdom is the ability to anticipate the consequences of a decision you make." These words
had an extraordinary meaning to me. I knew, based upon my years of
experience as a Commander, just how true and important the gravitas
of that statement was and continues to be. My prayers and hopes were
always that I could see things without blinders; I thought if I could forecast an issue or problem, I could proactively mitigate rather than reac-
tively minimize its impact, shield its effect, or mend its damage. I always

wanted to astutely anticipate consequences, accurately weigh risk, and construct good decisions.

Building one's competency is the absolute best practice in leadership; it builds unique knowledge, inimitable skill sets, and establishes functional and flexible abilities to successfully anticipate consequences, design plans, and implement strategies and tactics for successful results. Further, a leader's competence level increases her efficiency and effectiveness as a leader and efficacy as a manager.

I believe competence is illustrated by people who possess and demonstrate the knowledge, skills, and abilities to act correctly and effectively in a situational environment with a wide variety of facts and circumstances inside a particular set of task(s) and under the totality of understanding that those facts and circumstances are able to produce exemplary job performances and, by consequence, results.

I also believe that people cannot retain or sustain their competency without constant and ongoing development and growth.

I often told – and still tell – individuals God had blessed me with the discernment to not only understand how unimportant I am, but also how very important my role as a leader is. One's actions, behavior, conduct, and words send messages to others when he makes decisions and acts upon them. They also set his reputation among others in regards to his competency. The judgments made by those around him quickly solidify, translate into fact; they spread among the masses, among those he interacts with daily.

There are two extreme commonalities one often hears not only in the workplace, but, quite literally, everywhere. It's often something such as, "Oh, they are brilliant," or, "They don't have a clue." There is a huge benefit in the former and, obviously, not the latter. Perception – right or wrong – always trumps reality Competency is two pronged; first, the expertise required and needed in one's everyday craft contributes greatly to one's competency. Second, one's skills and abilities, the things that augment one's aptitude as a leader, are similarly important in cultivating and maintaining one's perceived competency. It is critically important for a leader to build and understand these two prongs while establishing reputation for his competency to be respected in both his craft and leadership.

Never be deceived by your angle of view that centers upon job knowledge, skills and abilities only, in other words the tip or "seen" portion of the ice berg of competency we label as "technical competencies". We need to see through the prism of totality to evaluate the "behavioral competencies" that include self-esteem, personality traits, desires and motives.

These "below the water line" competencies provide a picture that can forecast one's people skills and how they will interact and integrate into job frameworks, structures and systems with others.

It is an absolute burden to become competent, to maintain competency, and to sustain competence; because of the tremendous effort required to research and study, to maintain a working knowledge of oneself and chosen craft, one must invest her valuable time toward this endeavor every day. Today's leader must deliberately strive to remain proficient, confident, and felicitous in their craft.

The aptitude specific to one's job is tremendously, and pointedly, detailed and ever changing; this does not mention one's proficiency as Commander of staff and manager of organizational structures. Sonny Dixon, a friend and respected news anchor for WTOC television in Savannah, Georgia once quoted me a favorite saying of his grandfather's: "When you're green you grow, and when you're ripe you rot."

To remain green in today's world of turbulent mass communication, in-your-face multimedia, and ubiquitous and omniscient Internet access, one must intentionally strive to push forward and goal-seek daily. Constant and continuous research and study must be the normal course of duty if one means to stay current in her field and competent in her craft. Every opportunity for additional education and advancement of training and knowledge must be captured and used in the endeavor of becoming more learned and proficient in one's thought and critical decision processes.

37

As a Commander, people constantly will look to one for advice, guidance, and council regarding the issues afoot and problems arisen. They expect and demand one to first know, and second, be accurate and correct in his assessments and interpretations. One's people believe it is his ultimate responsibility to know and understand his job. Why? His authority and position. Such titles and constructs define the importance of knowing one's job and remaining contemporary.

Experience is a wonderful asset; however, experience alone will not bring one to her zenith any longer. One must strive to learn from others in her profession, through her experience, through her writings, and through her research. The ability to simply "keep up" can be and is daunting and labor intensive. The Internet is a double bladed sword: it acts, all at once, as invaluable resource and unbound harvester, an entity that will at once bestow upon you knowledge and ignorance.

The more proactive one is, the more prepared he will be to make decisions, implement them and manage the process. The better one improves his learning structure, the more he can be current. The problem lies here: change happens fast. Gaining accurate and factual information on which to base decisions – good decisions – often occurs only with the passage of time. Thus, frequently one will be arbitrarily judged over his lack of timeliness in the decision making process. The more current, self-confident, and comfortable in one's job he is, the more qualified and disciplined he will be as a decision maker.

When one is competent in her job, she demonstrates several behavioral patterns others immediately recognize. First, her self-confidence provides a certain calm and consistency. Second, her demeanor provides a needed and requisite credibility for those that follow her – often those same individuals want and desire to gain confidence themselves, even if never in a leadership capacity. Over time this pattern of consistency creates a positive reputation among others that she is very competent in her job and is, in fact, worthy to lead.

Such builds the reputation of character and trust for the knowledge and understanding of ability and proactivity does not stream forever on; at some point wisdom and character must manifest to sustain a Commander in the midst of his ever-changing world of responsibilities. However, a leader must, even through all these things, be competent and, most importantly, consistent.

Competency breeds consistency and followers love a consistent leader. Moreover, when one is consistent as a leader he creates an environment where those under his supervision are not scared to make decisions because they understand how to connect and think like their leader. Along with competency, consistency is a hallmark trait of great leaders. Further, the history of competency in an organization creates an environment amicable to and for decision-making. The historical course of resolutions, actions, and conducts build a blue print that one's followers find of great utility when they have to critically think.

Many CEO's will readily disclose that the most important attributes one can look for in a 21st Century employee are people skills and one's ability to think critically. A competent leader spawns and enhances her subordinate's abilities to think critically and deftly navigate any decision making process. Critical thinking begins with an assumption, evolves into a proposition, progresses through an analysis, then tumbles into evaluation, and ends in an argument based upon and rooted in facts and circumstances that support an accurate, hypothesis-backed conclusion. Key questions must be asked, facts must be established, and evidence must be weighed alongside objective application – humility also helps. Followers witness and mimic this process when they have the benefit of a competent leader.

The great teacher John Maxwell once said: "Poor leaders demand respect; competent leaders command respect." He's right; respect grows from others' understanding leader produced benefits from leaders who contain competency. As a leader, it is an absolute requirement to be secure in one's own shoes; he must be self-sure - competent; he must be self-confident – positive; he must be self-comfortable – keen; and he must be self-assured – imperturbable. If he embodies all these things, he will be prepared for the road to success.

But what about problems, kinks in the proverbial chain, or insecurities?

Mostly, organization-wide managerial problems and issues are most always rooted in one thing: insecurity. In fact, I believe the number one cause of micromanagement – that dirty word – is insecurity. Leaders who are insecure adversely impact those under their supervision, and, in reverse, their own bosses. Insecurity causes inaction – sometimes no-action – mediocrity, poor performance, and reactionary, or stagnant, operation. And what's the best way to combat this? Competence.

When leaders work to become and remain competent, they develop, grow, and perform their jobs at a much higher standard than others. These types of leaders possess an almost supernatural air, an aura that projects, exudes, and exemplifies their self-confidence and competence in all of their job duties. The way they act, talk, and interact with others demonstrates their talents and skill sets. Moreover, they develop a cred-ibility that causes others in any position around them to extend trust and respect.

This tri-base of support – subordinates, peers, and superiors – cre-ates an environment where one must be very comfortable in his ability to lead (influence) and manage (fulfill the responsibilities, obligations and functions of the job). This is critical to manage in a seamless posi-tion. Competence is the key element to obtaining this position in your organization.

To fully examine and accurately define competency in a glob-al fashion within the work place, one must focus on three important components.

First is leadership; agencies always reflect their leadership. The boss, the highest figurehead, casts the vision, creates the environment, and manages the process, while also influencing results and sustaining performances.

Second is the individual employee; good people with good skills and good work ethic translate into premier performance. The most valu-able resource and tool for either great success or absolute failure is the employee. Based upon their conducts, their behaviors, and their performances, efficiency and productivity are determined.

Third is organizational competency; policy and procedures, protocols and customs. These are the structures in place to guide and direct the required elements that insure credible, efficient, and effective operations

All three of these components must be factored into the overall equation of work place competency. It takes all three combined and blended together to create, develop, grow, and maintain the competencies needed in today's work place. This formula promotes the best practice, the best innovation, and the best results in all situations.

However, this wholesale package of competency is not free, not a gift or a shelved product to buy; one must earn it through dedicated devotion to duty and difficult, time-consuming hard work. Moreover, it never, ever stops, but remains ever-present, a continuous "burden" one must carry to always stay abreast, stay current, and stay capable in order to demonstrate good decision making prowess in combination with effective and meaningful actions that produce the best results not necessarily available, but always achievable.

Now, when one becomes the "boss," he has two huge choices that await him. He can be proactive, motivated, and industrious, be purposeful, exemplary, and meaningful. Or he can be reactive, stagnant, a backward thinker wasting time, resources and others' money, time, and lives forging a reputation that never will matter. The choice is his and fate rests in the balance.

If one chooses the former, then she must devote herself to nothing but the absolute best. Mediocrity and settling for the status quo are her enemies; premier performance, passion for excellence and being the best are her loving attributes. There is never enough time in the day to do it all, but one must find and reserve the time for her research and study, to the betterment of not only herself, but also her craft. Whether it's favorite Internet sites, professional organizations, periodicals, anecdotal coffee meeting, it's important to always strive for excellence.

I believe it is so tremendously important to merge the responsibility of personal development and grow with the counterpart of professionalism. It is difficult to separate one from the other. Moreover, we all know and recognize the facts regarding how much influence our beliefs have upon the way we think, frame issues, describe things, and ultimately decide issues and shape conduct and behavior. The way we think informs our mindsets, which, of course, are difficult to change.

The way we describe items and instances has a profound effect upon those we lead and others in our sphere of influence. We frame things based upon these descriptions and our framing has a tremendous impact upon those we command or influence. Framing highlights what we think is important or what we believe to be priority or, sometimes, what we believe and what we don't, what we determine as our truths, and what we determine as someone else's lie or misunderstanding. Even if we have the best intentions, our normative views, that we are smarter than the other, as a result our subjectively human beliefs, can triumph the objective truth. Thus, the more we can open our minds, the more enlightened we become, the better we will function both personally and professionally.

A very non-traditional means of training and education that has developed my knowledge base and the way others view issues and why has been National Public Radio and CNN. Both of these media sources have been huge for me to have the opportunity to learn at inopportune times. While riding down the road with public radio, to coming in late at night with CNN, both are there when I have time to be there.

These networks have been a tremendous resource for my personal and professional development and growth over the years. Not only have they educated me in both historic stories and current events, they have provided a source to hear and see the other side, others beliefs, others views that can be consistent or totally different from my own. Public radio has especially been beneficial because of the time they have to provide very specific background as well as their liberal slant that challenges my moderate leaning conservative position on most issues. My point is this: time used driving down the road listening to public radio educated me in many issues, opened my mind, broaden my views, and made me more knowledgeable about many issues; it motivated me to go dig deeper and further, to research and probe the issue that resulted in me becoming more fixed in my original thinking (knowing I was right), changing my mind, recognizing how difficult or near impossible it was to form a position, or just how dumb I was and unable to grasp it without seeking help.

In something as simple as handling media in my job, I have and still do gain a wealth of knowledge and "know how" that challenges my normative viewpoints, that keeps me on thinking, hypothesizing, and challenging myself. This self-challenging is an important key to becoming a great, respected leader.

But it's not just media. Technology has changed so much in such a short time; the availability and accessibility of information, the lightning speed of our communication, of our delineation of information, the frequency and volume of available knowledge, the intimacy and specifics of communication, and finally the storage and archiving of information in easily accessible nexuses has greatly enhanced one's ability to be more "in-tune" than ever before.

One can speak at a seminar, at a conference, in a classroom, or even from a bar stool and within minutes be revealed as a truth-sayer or an incompetent. Technologies, from portable smart phone applications for dictionaries, encyclopedias and compendiums, to automated GPS devices and "best-restaurant-in-five-blocks-finders," have facilitated vast and immediate data reach. I carry my entire Kindle library in my pocket; something that used to require a trip to my study simply requires a flick of the finger. Many applications from a "Google Alert" to "Flip-book" keep me situationally aware of the physical, political, and technological environment.

So what does this have to do with competency? With knowledge? With application? Everything. The point is this: wherever I go, whatever I do, I watch, listen, and learn. I take from everything some knowledge and I discern how to use it; I discern how to apply it to my work. Every competent leader must understand that anything and everything can and will teach him, inform him, mold him.

Great Commanders are excessively more motivated toward development and growth in their craft than toward their promotion or status in the organization. Personal and professional growth, alongside development, takes time, work, and dedication. Research and study are huge components to this effort. Thought, in combination with open-minded innovation, initiative, and opportunity augment this process. Research and study open doors to different perspectives, interpretations, and angles of view.

Many Commanders develop an experiential attitude, one that posits experience alone has brought them to where they need to be; but experience alone cannot be relied upon. Education and training is a must in a world where information and data change daily. The Commander must "stay up" to "keep up" and continuously strive toward growing his knowledge, enhancing his skills, and developing his abilities to exceed even the day before. One can never let himself be satisfied today without the knowledge of tomorrow.

Central to this concept is the understanding of the difference between what James Willis calls the "craft" and what he calls the "science;" Willis, in the police foundations publication "Improving Police: What's Craft Got to do With It?" defines and explores the differences between internal experience and external scientific study, and how both should be taken into thoughtful consideration and seen as a "marriage," or blend of practices, not two antagonisms at war with one another. It is clear that sometimes our entrenched views, solidified opinions, and well-intended methods may be wrong and that, perhaps, the evidence based other" is, in fact, correct.

The key is this: we come together with science and research to achieve the most reliable information available. So often we build our castles so high and dig our moats so deep that when we ought to be tearing down walls and draining moats to create an environment of mutual respect and open-mindedness, we devote far too much time toward the development of mis-ideas and inaccurate assessments. This, we cannot do. When craft and science merge together in a respectful and coordinated way, we all improve upon our competency.

One must set her schedules, plot her courses, and manage her shops in her own way; but she will always carry the burden to be better today than she was yesterday. 21st century organizations will not be kind to those who remain complacent in the workplace. The reactive and stagnant leader will not survive the results oriented and performance demanding, accountability dependent landscape of the 21st century. Only the proactive, visionary leader who works to be the best at her craft will survive and thrive well in the dynamic work environment of the 21st century.

But what is this craft I continually speak of?

The craft deals with those strategic, tactical, and technical aspects of one's job responsibilities. While organizational competency deals with one's leadership abilities and management skills within the organization in regards to the respect and reputation he enjoys from subordinates, peers and supervisors, organizational craft competency also involves excellent relationships and political capital within the agency. I use the term "political capital" to identify a cache of respect, organizational worth, and organizational value for the common good of the association, its core mission, and its necessary leadership.

"Political capital" develops from six factors:

1. **Loyalty:** Devotion and dedication to follow a leader's directional vision, to support every effort for the success and result that each leader strives to achieve.

2. **Work Ethic:** Deliberate and strive to do one's very best; perform one's job duties and responsibilities in an exemplary manner with 100 percent dedication and performance.

3. **Credibility**: Be always honest, truthful, and worthy to and for one's obligations.

4. **Reliability**: Trustworthiness and dedication to the right; do right, keep obligations first and above yourself.

5. **Performance:** Consistently work as hard as possible with exemplary effort.

6. **Results**: Resolution to achieve one's goals and objectives, to accomplish the requirements of every job and task.

The growth and development of your staff is integral in creating and sustaining a premier working staff. When one develops others, she acquires their trust, loyalty, respect, and passion to always please her in any and every endeavor they attempt. Moreover, they will make every attempt to emulate her skills, talents, and performances. They will even start thinking like her.

The absolute best way to obtain exemplary and outstanding performance, while mitigating or eliminating problems, minefields, pratfalls, and pitfalls lies in the investment one makes in his people's competencies. It is critical that he is self-confident and secure enough in himself to possess the ongoing determination to make those under his charge smarter and better than he is. Many insecure leaders see this as dangerous, stupid, and, frankly, working one's way out of a job; however, secure, servant-centered leaders see it as a huge advantage that creates a win/win situation for all involved. A visionary, purpose-driven leader will make tremendous effort and devote capital to mentor, coach, and embrace the apprentice in the work place.

One of the best tactics I have learned and used over the years in my mentorships of employees, and in my quest to improve their competencies and skill sets, is storytelling. Mornings around the coffee table were my time to gain interests, capture attention, inspire, motivate, and promote purpose and meaning. I would tell "war stories" with a teachable bent. I used this platform to stimulate emotion, promote thought, identify consequences, and produce vision.

Nonetheless, storytelling must be credible, articulate, and relevant to the listeners; it must tell the bad with the good, be specific and clear, and never let pride or vanity obfuscate its message. My best, most relatable stories revolve around my mistakes, times where I learned about work the ubiquitous "hard-way."

Storytelling is humane and pleasant because it displays and exhibits lessons without the sting of consequence that real experience produces on so many occasions. If one factors storytelling into his daily agenda, he can teach without effort regarding a multitude of various important subjects. Storytelling, in its essence, is organic training.

I remember when I commanded a drug task force and I used to worry about my agents doing a good job when planning and communicating with and for the unexpected during dynamic drug arrest situations. I would tell them the story of when I worked as an undercover agent for the G.B.I. in Atlanta, Georgia. Another agent and I were working a "buy-bust" – basically a sting – case near the General Motors (GM) plant in an Atlanta neighborhood. I would tell of how my partner and I met ahead of time with Atlanta police officers and other G.B.I. agents to plan the "buy-bust" and how the subsequent raid would go down. I related how our raid team took position using cover near the crowded and busy GM plant to waited for my signal to "come in fast," to affect the arrest, seize the dope, and cover us.

I told of how my partner and I left to go to the bad guy's house near the GM plant, and how we went inside a tense and dangerous situation with multiple bad guys. I told them when the main bad guy showed me the dope, I gave the code word over the hidden body transmitter I was wearing; the Atlanta Police Department and G.B.I. officers were supposed to rush in and arrest the bunch, but after three or four signals there was no response from our cavalry. All of a sudden, we heard a train whistle, that let us know that the G.M. vehicle train was between us and our raid team, thus our cavalry was on the other side of the tracks and could not get to us.

My story then escalated to the dangers we were exposed to by having to pull our guns and affect the arrest, outnumbered, and on the bad guys' turf. I told them how lucky we were and how great our relief was when our help was finally able to arrive. I used this "close call' to demonstrate to them the importance of planning and factoring in the environment and that a "plan B" in the event "plan A" becomes unavailable is paramount.

One must engage interests and promote thought among one's people, create an environment and promote an atmosphere of ideas, innovations, and consequence forecasting. Stress the importance of sharing instead of seeking – self-seeking – credit for completing the job alone. It's important to remember there is wisdom, not weakness, in reaching out for the assistance of others whom you know to be competent in the craft, excellent mentors, and trustworthy. Their important contribution adds to one's abilities and grows skills and abilities within her organization.

Recently, I attended a promotional reception for a friend of mine who is a picture perfect representation of competence, exemplary work ethic, and unwavering integrity. During the 2004 G-8 Summit, his reputation was forged throughout many local, state, and federal agencies for his textbook skills, usage and abilities to collaborate and partner with all stakeholders. The unique combination of his people skills, coupled with his no-nonsense dedication to protecting the security of our nation, made him a paragon leader in such an important and high profile event. Through servant-hood and competence, his reputation followed him as he climbed his organization's ladder. His name is Mark Giuliano and he is the Assistant Director of the F.B.I.

During Mark's address in his recent reception in Atlanta, he reemphasized a belief he holds true and lives through his work: "We are better working together, than we are working apart." His message highlighted the value of collaboration in today's work place; other professionals have great ideas and innovations that can develop and grow one's organization. Moreover, sometimes these people see what some don't; however this information is necessary for all.

Another important component used to assist the leader in the goal of development and progress of their staff is providing them with additional competent role models to mentor to them. These mentors need to share the same values, work ethic, vision, and skills as the leader. In other words, they need to share the leader's vision for the overall "cultural development "of the work place. Above all they must be competent in their craft and how they teach followers. Additional mentors will later spawn from within; the experience of the staff as a product of the whole culture and process of coaching, mentorship, and teaching ultimately leads to this.

Tom Davis, a dear friend and fabulous investigator in the G.B.I., was instrumental in my responsibility to create, design, build, and implement a multi-jurisdictional task force. The unique combination of his sense of purpose, passion for his work, and superior talents and competencies was a tremendous asset toward the task force's ability to develop and grow its agents and later produce many great state and federal agents. Tom did not mirror me, I didn't want him too; he had his particular way of doing things, a way that sometimes differed from mine. However, his ways, like my ways, were always moral, legal, and ethical. Moreover, our beliefs, values, cultural mores, and standards were the same.

Thus, the vision matched as well. My subordinates grew from Tom's mentorship and so did I, not to mention the profound positive effect he had on our task force and the exemplary results the task force had in its job. I could not have done what I had to do without him in the role of a mentor to my people, his infectious passion for the work, his candid advice to me, and his expertise that made everyone better.

Again, drug enforcement can be more of an art than a science; it's a cat and mouse mentality. Dependence upon either raids or undercover tactics promotes a particular selection of myriad choices as any particular strategy at any particular time. Marty Zon, another dear friend and one of the best narcotic agents I ever knew, led one of the most success-ful drug task forces in the history of Georgia and taught those around him that when it came to planning strategy and implementing tactics for undercover operations, there was and is no "cookie cutter" solution, no one answer in this arena of policing. There always was and is another option to examine and weigh. This demonstrates why it is so important to expose one's people to other ideas, views, and thought processes from other competent mentors, technologies, and teachings.

Ideas are developed from the God-given benefit of the constructive thought process in conjunction with the innate abilities to deduction, deduce-ment, and intention. Ideas fuel innovations and promote posi-tive changes that can benefit everyone in the organization. The most difficult part comes in translating those ideas into plans, strategies, tac-tics, and projects that are creative and valuable. Transitions and trans-formations require tremendous vision and exemplary leadership. This is true especially in the light of any new and innovative initiative one may produce and apply in her work.

The very first rules of business in this effort are the design, construc-tion, and creation of a structured framework to work within in order to insure competency, clarity, and consistency. One never wants to let the horse out of the barn without first building a fence. Things go astray when allowed to evolve on their own. In the late 80's and early 90's, the Department of Justice awarded grants for the organization and imple-mentation of multi-jurisdictional drug task forces to combat the plague of drug distribution throughout the country. This very meaningful and important program was named after Eddie Byrne, a hero who had given his life as a New York Police Officer. These grant funds provided drug enforcement relief to many areas where none existed before. In Georgia, many local agencies applied for and received these grant awards to start up these task forces.

Drug enforcement, unlike many routine functions in police work, requires specific competencies and particular expertise in many dif-ferent areas such as search and seizure, evidence room management, informant files, covert investigative fund distribution, and accounting. Many of these first task forces appointed Commanders from rural areas with good work ethic or political influence. Seldom were they trained or prepared for the new duty requirements and accounting skills necessary to perform and maintain adequately the responsibilities placed upon their shoulders; as a result, many of these task forces quickly fell into trouble; lost or mishandled evidence; unaccounted funds; less than professional tactics.

At the time, the then Governor's criminal justice coordinating council controlled these grant distributions and made it a point to highly encourage the use of GBI supervisors as task force Commanders of these organizations. However, this effort was not pushed because the GBI was better or more suitable. This incorporation of GBI supervisors was favored due to GBI having a detailed policy and specific procedures for drug enforcement administration, logistics and operations.

The bottom line: the GBI had a tested and proven structure in place for Commanders to use as a guide in their management efforts. These GBI supervised task forces operated well when regular oversight insured compliance with the structures in place. Thus, the importance of "structure," alongside well-crafted policy, one taught and aggressively supervised, made its central behavior a part of the workplace culture. The horse now had a fence.

When Sheriff Randall Tippins appointed me Chief Deputy Sheriff of Evans County, he outlined his vision for where he wanted his agency to go. He wanted to seek grant funding and to employ intelligence-based information and guided operations into the agency. We were able to secure vital federal funding to construct, from the ground up, an intelligence led policing program different from any in the country. Our program established a position of a full time intelligence analyst to spearhead our efforts for transitional and transformational endeavors in a new and innovative landscape rarely seen in an agency of our size. Moreover, this transformation positively affected the local police departments, neighboring municipalities, and state and federal partners as well. We created and constructed systems and networks to promote the sharing and dissemination of information to facilitate the operations results.

Due to divine intervention and funds from the department of homeland security, Dr. David Carter, the "master" of intelligence function, and later primary mentor of ours, was teaching a class at the Desoto Hilton in Savannah. This "Intelligence Tool Kit" class was attended by Sheriff Tippins, our analyst Bryant Jones, and I. We learned about the benefits of proper intelligence operations in conjunction with the rich history of failures, tribulations, and civil liabilities associated with such aspirations. Further, we learned the benefits of a sound and specific privacy policy to guard and secure people's civil rights and the importance of detailed procedures regarding the federal rules of 28 CFR 23 – a rule that protects people's constitutional rights and an agency's credibility – in intelligence operations.

After Dr. Carter's class, I knew I had to dig further and farther to achieve the competencies I needed, that Randall required, and that Bryant needed for the proper supervision of design and development of a modern, 21st century, Intelligence Led Policing operation, something that could be narrowly tailored for a small rural agency, yet broad enough to be interoperable to a large metropolitan agency. Dr. Carter and the department of Homeland Security provided the foundation, but I would be responsible for the specific design, materials list, labor, and construction. I knew what I had to do: research, network and study.

I used the Internet, through its credible websites, to read and study specific details regarding particular issues, opinions, and "lessons learned." Then I work called various subject matter experts around the country to get candid commentary on my assumptions. I read books and compared data from various government organizations dedicated to the promotion of intelligence operations. I also talked to the road deputies and subordinate officers to ensure any procedure design or policy development started was being built from the ground up. I especially found this helpful when trying to understand modern technologies and how they can be applied into the operational plans. I found out again how important it was to improve my knowledge inventory on technology and how that improved process would (like the technology) be ever changing and evolving, thus the requirements for me to ensure I stayed up to speed.

Now, I know the importance of having people on one's staff with the requisite expertise, but the Commander must possess a working knowledge that can provide a contextual and working understanding of new and evolving technologies, concepts, or ideas. This is a requirement for the vast autobahns of information that snake across the 21st century environment.

I continued to research, read, study, evaluate, and network and found this to be the recipe for absolute success, one that prepared me to work with everyone involved to design and implement procedures and systems. We, our team, knew we must have our policy and procedures in place before we started the operation. Thanks to our mentor and advisor Dr. Carter and our sheriff's disciplined leadership to wait until ready, we became uniquely qualified to start our program. Then, as a result of everyone's collaboration, we were selected by the Bureau of Justice assistance as being one of the top ten best practices for intelligence led policing in the Country.

In closing, I firmly believe that one must always "put the horse before the cart" and be prepared to understand as much as he can and, when possible, seek out and put in place a structure or framework to operate within. This is as much a part of the overall formula for success as the key competencies possessed by individuals in the organization. Knowing as much as one can, as soon as one can, is crucial, but what one knows needs to be both accurate and current within the context of the situation afoot. Thus, education is necessary, at least in some capacities.

One's habits of listening, questioning, digesting, objectively evaluating, and learning are tremendously important in his quest to gain competency and sustainability in quality through any situation. Moreover, if one knows but does not act the way he understands he should, his opportunity to demonstrate his competence is lost. One must be able to know his course, and then have the fortitude, courage, and discipline to follow it.

"Competency is the wisdom to know and the discipline to behave consistently with that knowledge to drive conduct"

We possess wisdom with what we know, and our ability to anticipate the consequences for our actions sets us apart. We will always be judged by what people believe we know or what they believe we should know. We make decisions, initiate, or approve plans and actions or stand silent, turn blind eyes to actions, conducts, behaviors, or events around us: the choice is ours.

We measure what is reasonable or proper based upon what we know at the time. Thus, it is so tremendously important for us to be well educated, prepared, and aware of the world around us. Change is quick, it doesn't wait, and it doesn't rest. Our greatest hurdle is realizing this.

We demonstrate competency with how we apply what we know to what we do.

We are measured by our ability to develop solutions, provide good advice, and match our knowledge with our conduct and behavior while performing our duties and fulfilling our responsibilities.

A central component of the formula used by others to judge our competency is our ability to grow and develop others around us. To accomplish this task we must not only know our stuff and translate our knowledge into exemplary performance, but also teach others around us by example and mentorship. The requirement to promote wisdom and understanding regarding our craft is tremendously important for all Commanders. The professional growth and development of one's subordinates is paramount to building her influence and credibility of those subordinates' leader; fulfilling one's obligation as a Commander to the organization and the mission by producing the best job performance possible also ranks highly on the leader's list.

Professional growth and development is a fluid concept where information gained leads to new or different ideas, perspectives, or angle sof view that identify priorities, shapes, or recalculations of policy in framing and focus. Further, this developmental growth process enables one to proactively plan and correctly react for and to the ever changing situations, incidents, and events in the environment of their professional responsibilities and required duties.

This "culture" of situational awareness that is a product of this developmental growth promotes and enhances premier decision-making. Moreover, I am convinced that the more competencies a leader can develop and nurture, the more he mitigates the risk of his personal feelings, pride, or ego defeating his ability to see, assess, and evaluate internal and external issues objectively when required, thus creating an adaptive organizational environment resistant to failures resulting from subjective mind sets and a command or institutionalized arrogance toward changing direction. Creating, developing, and growing individual competency builds and develops work place competency for all staff.

I believe building work place or work unit competencies can be defined best by Dr. Dusya Vera and Dr. Mary Crossan as "[the] process of change in thought and action – both individual and shared – embedded in and affected by the institutions of the organizations." The cornerstone to competency lies in our skills in gathering, interpreting, and accurately understanding facts and circumstances around us, how those facts relate to and shape the current landscape of issues, events, and ideas, and how we incorporate those facts into our own ideals and everyday frameworks. Central to this process is the self-discipline to fight the human condition and emotional tendency to rush to judgments without the benefit of all the facts. The urge and momentum to jump to conclusions regarding any issue remains as a perpetual impediment to accurate and objective assessments of issues and events in life.

Thus, we must fight to condition ourselves and discipline our thought processes to follow a reasonable path to objectively fact-find, objectively evaluate, and objectively understand all issues in a global perspective.

Time can be our worst enemy or our best ally, and it all depends upon the totality of each fact, set, and circumstance. We may have to act quickly or risk losing the initiative. Such is based upon the facts of each case and the specifics of the content and context of the information involved.

To determine the veracity or accuracy of any story or information provided to me, I always start by asking one of the most important questions any leader can ask: "How do you know?" It requires of the person asked to give an account of their basis of knowledge. This leads to the identification of sources, establishment of specific details and particular facts, and elucidation of circumstances. This degree of specificity is necessary to insure the reliability and credibility of one's information.

Use of the question in combination with a protocol that follows a systematic evaluation plan in regards to information will mitigate risk, prevent problems, and enhance chances for successful and accurate conclusions. Moreover, the notion of seeking specificity from all sources leads to a Commander's most cherished fact-finding skill, the ability to form the next question. Such processes prepare one to make and benefit from good decision making due to having the most accurate and complete information.

The system I use follows seven basic steps:

1. Be skeptical of first impressions; reserve judgment when without benefit of all the facts

2. Aggressively listen to everyone. Everyone.

3. Ask specific and probing questions, especially, "How do you know?"

4. Be skeptical as information develops; always objectively evaluate facts with an open mind.

5. Draw inferences or conclusions based upon and supported by facts.

6. Anticipate unintended consequences.

7. Sustain an environmental awareness.

Moreover, remember the all-important "**RRSEN**" acronym:

RESEARCH: Dig through the Internet, professional periodicals, and journals to identify and gather information; drill down specifics.

READ: Absorb and process information.

STUDY: Digest information and ensure possession of the accurate and thorough working knowledge of the subject matter.

EVALUATE: Use thoughtful analysis to compare and contrast facts and information; play devil's advocate with assessments; look at the facts from different perspectives and angles of view.

NETWORK: Discuss issues with others such as subject matter experts, peers, academics and the outstanding people who are responsible for the work to be done. Remain opened minded and listen to everyone.

Always remember to listen to the opposite view, consider the other side, be open-minded, and, most importantly, do not fall into the pattern trap of "occupational arrogance," a malaise that forms within the innate human tendency to become fixed in one, comfortable belief. It is a burden to become competent and to sustain that competence, but it is an absolute requirement when one is responsible for work results, responsible for developing and growing individuals as integral parts to the success of an organization and exemplary performance toward the purpose of that organization's mission.

There are 3 keys to developing and maintaining the ability to be competent:

- Sustain a proactive mindset toward remaining current in your craft, driven by research, study and preparation.

- Maintain a constant state of humility and listen to others.

- Keep the self-discipline to always let the facts lead your thought process and decision making over your emotions.

Chapter Three

"THE BURDEN OF SERVANT-HOOD"

The real question is: do you possess the self-confidence, humility and self-discipline to make sacrifices for those under your charge... can you put them before you?

"So if I, your Lord and Teacher, have washed your feet, you also ought to wash one another's feet. For I have set you an example that you also should do as I have done to you."
John 13: 14-15 NRSV

The absolute key to the ability of the Commander to sustain the skills necessary to maneuver competently through the responsibilities associated with the management of people is the surrender to the paradigm of servant-hood tailored and clothed in humility. This is an incredibly difficult thing to do, beyond the instincts of our human nature. We are inherently selfless, greedy, and egotistical with a built in tendency of insecurity and paranoia, especially when relating to those that may be of potential competition.

This ingrained streak of the self-centered "me" attitude is the fuel for negative thoughts and mindsets, and it is a huge factor in how we frame issues. Thus, this attitude designs our behavior and conduct, how we perceive and treat others. Further, how we perceive and treat others sets the stage for our ability to manage and lead, and funnels directly to our efficacies as Commanders.

If we can fight the natural "automatic pilot" of the "human condition," the one that thrives upon being selfish and self-centered, and instead carry the burden by forcing ourselves to into the role of the servant leader, one with genuine care and concern for those under his charge, then and only then can we possess the skill sets to command effectively and efficiently.

My mother used to say, "Never brag on yourself. If you do, well, others will know it and talk about it." I've found this to be the absolute truth.

I've learned and am firmly resolved to the fact that the most important thing one can do is never take credit, but always give credit. Always put the light on the other person. Humility is the greatest asset a leader can have in this, and any, arena. Humility bestows one with the capacity to give credit and deposit relational currency. Harry Truman once said: "It is amazing what you can accomplish if you do not care who gets the credit."

One must work to maintain and sustain humility, especially in an organizational context. Oftentimes, the higher one rises, the harder it becomes to insure this precious state of humility. My 36 year career has taught me that everything that one does will, in some way, come back to him. What returns to one, if he chooses to be a servant leader, is love, respect, loyalty, reputation, and tons of credit. I believe this notion to be equally important in both the government and public sectors the business and private zones.

Two men, one from the public sector and one from the private sector, embody this ideal completely: Charles Sikes, Retired Special

Agent in Charge, Georgia Bureau of Investigation, and Ellis Wood, CEO, Ellis Wood Contracting, respectively. Both of these men do what all servant leaders do, or should do: they model their servant centered and unselfish behavior in front of the world, yet in a modest and humble fashion.

Charles Sikes, a former supervisor and mentor of mine, showed me the true benefits of servant leadership through his vision and selflessness. Charles had a saying: "horses and troops eat before the officers." I found this to be incredibly good and poignant advice. Charles knew that denying himself enhanced others. He took the best equipment last, the worst seat, was the last in line. Charles knew the benefits one could and would receive by living this message; he only solidified it by living it, thus he demonstrated stellar leadership.

Ellis Wood, a great entrepreneur and philanthropist who served became a role model through his humility, demonstrated time and time again the importance of nobility and honor, that by walking in those things one understands how to deny himself and uplift others. Ellis would take his personnel and equipment, on his dime, to communities throughout the state to clear damage and clean private property for people he did not know, after tornadoes or terrible storms. He took care of his own employees the same way, always being there for them, helping at times of need. His financial resources went to others when they could have gone to him alone. Such sacrifice demonstrated to all around him why one could not only trust and respect him, but certainly follow him.

However, the greatest example comes from Jesus Christ, the greatest leader I believe the world has ever known, a figure who represents everyone; He washed his disciples' feet instead of letting them was his feet. Such was his message regarding the importance of the leader's first and foremost responsibility to become a servant to his followers.

Poet T.S. Eliot said: "Half of the harm that is done in this world is due to people who want to feel important…they do not mean to do harm… they are absorbed in the endless struggle to think well of themselves."

But I think John Maxwell puts it best: "As you rise in leadership, responsibilities increase, and rights decrease...You lose the right to put yourself first". Wow, how could it ever be put better? As Commanders we lose the right to use our position to go first and be first; others do and must take priority.The true measure of servant-hood manifests when one risks himself over something that he doesn't have to. He exposes himself to disfavor or criticism from his "boss" over something he does for someone else.

I remember a time where a young agent that was transferred to our work unit from Atlanta headquarters came into my office with a long face, nervous demeanor, and limited eye contact. He said, "Boss, I've got a problem."

I told him to come in and talk with me about it. He sat reserved and uneasy while I sat at my desk. "What's the problem?" I asked. He replied that it was about his gun. My heart sank and I quickly grew nervous; my first thought was that it was stolen; my second it was lost, and my third, the worst, pawned. Any bad thing about an officer's gun was and isn't good; it usually began with an investigation, then turned into paper-work, then disciplinary action.

I quickly said, "Tell me about it."

"It's my serial number," he said.

My heart sank again; I asked what was wrong with the serial number and he replied, "666; it's the devils number." I slid back into my seat with a great degree of calmness, my fears assuaged; it was almost comical, at first. Then I read his face and watched his demeanor; I immediately knew that I needed to take this as serious.

My faith would prevail over a 666 label – I wouldn't like it – but I know my business with the good Lord is in line and straight up. However, this agent was clearly disturbed and adversely impacted. Moreover, he was worried sick and scared to death. I knew then that if this issue was that important to him, it better become real important to me. The question quickly became, "How am I going to deal with this?"

At this time, my boss was a no nonsense critical opponent of anything that produced or promoted extra work or additional efforts. He wasn't known to be particularly sensitive to the feelings of others. He was a highly competent, fiercely hardworking, and extremely ambitious guy who wanted to climb to the top of the organization. We saw a lot of things exactly alike, but we also had differences in our management philosophies. I considered him a friend and he appreciated the fact I was unwaveringly loyal to him.

I knew to trade a perfectly functioning and reliable Glock 40 pistol meant a bevy of paperwork, a specific – and arduous – approval process, and time and money-cost of a complete swap. This wasn't to mention the precedence such action would create under his watch. However, I knew how important this was to the one under my watch, and that was my responsibility, to fix things. Subordinates look to the "boss" to fix things and care for them. This is as much a requirement for being the "boss" as anything else in management. I knew if I flinched, chickened out, or welched on this subordinate's behalf, he would be devastated, and I would be seen as worthless and untrustworthy. I knew I had a responsibility to care, act, and fix his problem. So I did.

Many times one can talk through an issue, de-escalate it, defuse it, postpone action, or eliminate the problem altogether to the acceptance, approval, and satisfaction of one's subordinate. Other times, one absolutely cannot; the opportunity simply does not exist. Whether it be due to passion or determination, obstacles or unforeseens, sometimes the cards are stacked wrong. This was clearly such a case; this employee's belief was so ingrained that nothing would suite him other than to be rid of this gun, a gun he saw as a sign and curse.

Thank goodness I had learned the rules of what John Maxwell calls "leading up;" I had invested the time, the work, and the requisite relational and depository performance with my own "boss" to have the interpersonal clout to call in a favor. So, with my hat in my hand, I made the call and heralded the plea for the gun swap. Armed with the proposition that I would do all the work, lay the logistical course, and incorporate multitasking to cover other needed responsibilities – what mama called killing two birds with one stone – I made my case.

My "boss" laughed and gave me a mulligan approving the trade, with some reservation reserved in later commentary. My "boss" gave me an opportunity to build credibility and forge trust and respect. Why? Because I had done the same with him.

My subordinate now knew I would put him before me; he was smart enough to know the issues and the playing field upon which I had to operate. He saw me adopt his problem, embrace his cause, and put myself on the line for him. I knew this would – and it did – reap huge benefits in my leadership and management of this agent. From that day, he saw me as a servant leader and knew if I stuck by him on this issue, I would be with him on any other.

On another occasion, opportunity to demonstrate servant leadership came once again; this time my "boss" was present and part of the equation regarding how and where priority could be placed.

It was a great day at the office, everything was running well; our Deputy Director was visiting, and I was in deep conversation with him when one of my agents approached me, red faced, openly nervous, and emotionally upset.

I asked the Director to excuse us, and I walk with the agent to his office. I asked what was wrong; he was livid and his voice cracked as he told his story. He advised that some four months prior he had booked a cruise through the Caribbean with his wife, had purchased two very expensive nonrefundable tickets for the journey. He related that before he planned the trip he had called all four jurisdictions of the District Attorneys' Offices and told them of his plans. He continued by stating that he had gained their assistance in working around their county court calendars and schedules so he would not be impacted or impact any court schedules should an appearance be required or subpoena issued. All administrators' at all four offices gave him a green light for his dates and told him he would be fine to plan his trip. Then, all of a sudden, - of course, things like this always seem to happen –he gets a subpoena that very morning for court on the day his was supposed to be on vacation.

Now I knew and understood very well that if one is subpoenaed for court, he must honor the subpoena and appear. Historically, our job requires us to cancel plans in order to serve the wishes of a prosecutor or judge. Therefore, I knew this may be a battle I could not win. However, win or lose, I knew I had an obligation and duty to try my absolute best for this employee, one who had busted his tail for me and his organization and had, in his defense, gone through the proactive and appropriate channels to prepare an adequate schedule.

I knew what I had to do; I walked down the hall and told the Deputy Director that with all due respect, I had to leave with our agent to eliminate a problem beyond his ability to handle. I told the agent to meet me in the parking lot.

While driving from the office, I told him we were going to meet with the prosecutor and speak with him. If that did not work, we would have an audience with the judge; I planned to request to one, or both if necessary, to move the case to another date. We met with the prosecutor, and the prosecutor conferred with the judge; ultimately, the court was postponed until our agent returned from his vacation.

I left my big "boss" to be an advocate for my subordinate, to do whatever I could in my power to help him out of his situation. Now, everyone around the office knew what had happened. Consequently, my Deputy Director understood my responsibility and my actions. This translated to a relational currency account that grew with this agent and his wife, and my "boss."

It's not an accident that Jesus washed the disciples' feet. It is a common theme seen time and time again throughout history, when true leaders demonstrate the unadulterated essence of leading. When one really cares, she truly bears the burden of command to insure her people come first. She takes responsibility for them because she feels ownership in them, and when they develop and perform well, she feels good about what she's done.

So what does a servant leader look like and what do they do? What makes them different? First, they empower; second, they mentor; third, they command accountability for results and performance; fourth, and finally, they dole credit.

But out of these four features, I've identified seven absolute traits of servant leaders:

1. They believe in purpose and model that belief to and for their people:

Purpose is one of the strongest motivators available; vast majorities of individuals work for and embrace purposeful endeavors in life. Purpose can trump money, status, and other human motivators in today's work place. When a Commander incorporates "purpose" into his mission, and casts that vision regularly among his staff, such action will create an environment of meaningful work and consequential job importance. This increases motivation to not only do the job, but also enjoy it and do it well.

In order for those one leads to "buy in," to "join in" to this process, they must see sincerity, credibility, and edification that this cannot and will not happen if the Commander does not demonstrate and display such dedication and devotion to "purpose" every day. The Commander, through his leadership skills, must talk the talk that matches their walked walk. In order for the subordinates to believe, they must see and trust that the Commander believes in the mission and purpose, and that he strives toward its requirements, responsibilities, goals, and objectives. One must sell purpose, advocate its importance, embrace its means, and work toward its fulfilment.

2. Preach and cast vision toward shared purpose; illuminate how individuals will play major roles in realizing vision.

One must incorporate her subordinates into the formula to promote purpose and achieve worthwhile benefits from exemplary work results. This takes an active and persistent presence on her part to remind those working under her charge of the importance of what they do – no matter how small – and how such importance of action will lead to success. They must know that their role, that their responsibility, and that their work is important and meaningful. This means she, the leader, must be there to remind them and encourage them.

3.   Provide clear, unambiguous expectations.

One's people must also know the best way to get it done; this may be from past experience, new practices, new teachings, or new ideas or even relational building collaboration between leader and subordinate. Everything from risk to reward factors into this equation and depends upon the nature of the task that may be, depending on circumstance, limited or unlimited in methods or means to proceed.

However, central to this effort is one's responsibility to provide clear and understandable expectations regarding what he expects from his subordinates, even as minutely as how they go about the job. One never micromanages them; he can give them the hymnal, page number, song and verse, but he always let them do the singing.

4.   Empower people; delegate responsibilities and allow ownership.

My daddy provided me an old car when I was 16; it was a 1966 Volkswagen Bug. He told me that I could save my money from working at the grocery store to buy a nicer used car later. I needed a set of tires and asked daddy if he would buy them for me. He was quick to say no; he went on to say that if I paid for the tires myself, I would be less likely to "burn rubber" or spin wheels because it would "come out of my pocket."

I found this to be sound advice. I saw a lot of tire spinning from those on their "dad's bill."

Here's my point: we know that when people "own" something they tend to take care of it better. We also know that if people "own" something, whether tangible or intangible, and they do something good with that "ownership," they feel good, it builds confidence and self-esteem alongside pride and ambition to succeed. Sometimes they even compete to become "better" or, ultimately, the "best."

From the racehorse one owns, to the idea from which she creates, ownership makes things a part of the psyche, it factors into the emotional draw of being human. When good things happen because of us, it makes us feel important. And let's face it: everyone wants to be important.

When one delegates and gives someone ownership, that something, whatever it may be, becomes theirs; most of the time they will treat it better and work harder for it because it reflects directly upon them whether it's successful or not. This is why it is so important to delegate to those under one's command and allow them to succeed. When they accomplish the task they own, they feel a sense of great accomplishment and build their confidence and abilities at the same time for the next task or mission.

One must let them do it and give them the full credit when they do. One must never micro-manage them; one's job is to prepare them by providing training, casting vision, and sustainable mentorship, then give them clear unambiguous expectations along with the resources required to meet those expectations; The final step? Release them to do it.

But always remember this: be there if they need you and always let them do it.

5. Encourage; brandish the mantle of mentor; continually support efforts.

Be there for them twenty-four-seven. Be there by phone, text, e-mail; be available for them no matter what. Take interest, touch base, encourage; let them know they have you and you have faith in them. Do not overlook their poor performances, their mistakes, or their sometimes-poor decision making; correct them in a private setting and in such a fashion that lets them know you or others have made the same mistakes. Correct in a positive way that nurtures developmental growth in a productive manner. Encourage them always; praise their efforts when worthy, but also demand professionalism. Commend them on excellent results.

6. Accept responsibility for actions, both one's own and others'.

The "buck stops with you;" the commander is responsible when things go bad. Never look to place blame, but always accept responsibility. Look in the mirror, at yourself, not out the window hunting your subordinates for the plumpest one to take the fall. Back your people and they will develop the fortitude to make decisions themselves, grow in maturity and leadership qualities. Moreover, when your people see that their success and growth and development as an employee overrides your ambitions as commander, they will die for you. Remember, the difference between operational or administrative mistakes and mishaps and illegal, unethical, or unprofessional conduct. Never support non-professional conduct or behaviors; always preach professional standards and enact zero tolerance policies for improper and unprofessional behavior.

7. Praise; give all the credit.

Never, ever take credit; give your people all the credit. Be modest and humble, and do everything in your power to make them shine. Praise them in a public or open setting, and encourage their behavior by being specific about what they did right. Be sincere at all times and genuinely take joy in their accomplishments.

For the ability to delegate duties and receive exemplary results, leaders must be able to release people under their command to do the work, make decisions, receive latitude to operate as they see fit within the policy-centric, professional standards required by the job. In order for people under your charge to make those decisions, take risks, and seize opportunities, they must know that if they make mistakes, you will back them and not throw them under the bus.

Often, self-serving ambition can be your greatest impediment and most incorrigible ally.

Have you ever had a boss who talked about "when they get to be Major or Chief or Director," or "how they are going to get to the top?" This rhetoric translates into the functional equivalent of saying: "I'll do what I need to do to get there, including not taking the heat for your mistakes."

One's people must see a leader who centers upon, talks about, cares about, and wants to see them succeed and climb the organizational ladder. When they see that the leader that puts them first, they know they have a person that will back them and take responsibility for their actions. They also know they are sincere about employee development and growth within the organization.

Mentorship must be genuine and sincere and coupled with the common goal to exceed in work performed. The mentor relationship is based upon four components: belief in mission and purpose; competence in the job; genuine care and commitment toward the apprentice; and encouragement through pride in the apprentice's work.

Mentorship must be proactive in nature; this means showing one's people what to expect, illustrating examples of job issues, promoting consequence-thinking, and telling of "war stories," of past events and incidents relevant to current scenarios or climates. Self-confident servant leaders can openly talk about their experiences, their past failures and mistakes, and use these stories as "teachable moments." I've learned over the years how valuable these moments can be and how meaningful they are when provided by the Commander with the transparent intent to save subordinates from making similar mistakes or experiencing the same failures.

These proactive opportunities of demonstration to those under one's charge are tremendously important in building a competent and highly skilled staff. Mentors also search, locate, and secure good training for their people. Training removes staff from their normative environment and causes the Commander to either tell others to take their place or the do the additional work themselves. Thus, training can and does become an impediment, especially in a resource-stressed work environment. However, I have always found that one may hurt today, but be better tomorrow for benefits of training. Successful Commanders know that investment in training pays big dividends to the work place performance.

A central tenet to mentorship is to instill in one's people self-confidence tempered with humility and clothed with constant and objective self-evaluation. Mentorship is the tool the commander uses to nurture, develop, and grow the organization's greatest resource – people – further; this molding process shapes the "culture" of the work place.

The last chapter stressed the importance of competency and to function well as a servant-leader, one needs to build his competence in his craft. So much of true servant-leadership is devoted to the growth and development of others. To teach, one must know his subject matter. With subject matter knowledge, practical experience, and a passion to teach, a leader can become an excellent mentor to those under his charge. Knowing one's material and transparently sharing how and why such material is important to the development of the team are crucial and important steps the Commander must take in their quest to be a servant leader and outstanding manager.

In today's world of do more with fewer resources and more responsibilities in less time, supervisors often can't or do not set aside the time to put forth the effort to mentor. Mentorship is the best proactive programing to prevent and mitigate risk and eliminate problems while enhancing performance. Mentorship requires time, dedication, patience, and hard work. Moreover, mentorship must become an ingrained culture within the work place for all to fully embrace.

As a mentor, one can never walk past poor performance; she must deal with adverse issues when they happen to improve future conduct. Always correct in private and praise in public to preserve self-esteem and promote pride in one's work. Remember to address the conduct and behavior only and never attack or degrade the individual person. Provide specific examples of how the improper conduct adversely affects the mission, and explain the consequences involved. Then give examples of the correct method or manner needed to be followed and solicit always feedback.

Always remain receptive to new ideas or ways of doing work; I remember as a young boy my father showing me how to shell peas under the car port. He would carefully demonstrate exactly how to rip the inner stem and use your two thumbs to pressure each pea from its pod. After learning his process, I developed my own way that I thought was both easier and quicker. Once my father caught me deviating from his method he quickly directed me to shell them the way he had taught me. When he would leave to go back into the house, I went back to shelling the peas my way. Both ways achieved the same result. Your footsteps do not always have to be followed exactly; others will have their "particular ways" of doing things. As long as the job gets done in an effective and competent manner and with the positive and worthwhile results, sometimes it may not manner how we got there.

In the chapter regarding the burden of competency, I outlined the importance of the Commander staying abreast of the latest information involving his craft. I went on to talk about the obligation the leader has toward his people to be competent and remain competent. Now, I have to take this idea to another level, one that increases the burdens placed upon the Commander; this level requires that the Commander's responsibility go beyond traditional personal mentorship and climb to the intended regular sharing of craft competency information through the same resources I wrote about in the burden of competency – e.g. technology, self-teaching, etc.

The Commander must ensure that when she receives or is exposed to new information through her constant research, she must also share and prepare her subordinates always. This exercise in additional work is difficult and labor intensive, but it is an investment in one's people that will pay big dividends toward better performance and the mitigation of risk and problems.

Remember the value and importance of setting specific and unambiguous expectations and making sure those expectations are communicated well and understood fully. One must develop the fortitude and courage to insure she provides objective, honest, and credible performance evaluations regarding those she mentors. If one coaches, supervises, manages, and mentors correctly, her subordinates are never surprised and continually know what to expect during an evaluation; they also understand why. When someone is disciplined, they are never surprised if the Commander has done her job correctly.

Many managers wait until evaluation time to deal with performance issues and such is an absolute disaster. Evaluations should be conducted daily, with foci on performance improvement and problem prevention. or insure you have done absolutely everything possible to savage an employee before you have to jeopardize their employment. Mentorship is a process that fuels and sustains accurate evaluations and prepares the way for an evaluation to be properly utilized.

Moreover, you bring credibility to your organization because you will ensure the paper evaluation matches the informal talk and reputation. Far too many organizations have managers that do not document accurate and truthful evaluations. This causes significant problems for the entire organization from promotions to discipline. Those under one's command deserve to know when they do right and when they do wrong, they deserve this critique in a timely and proactive fashion where there is sufficient time to change their conduct and behavior.

Many things factor into one's ability to change their ways. First, they have to see and understand what went wrong or right. Second, they need to possess the knowledge, skills, and/or abilities to change. Third, they must have feedback, coaching direction, encouragement, and praise. The first two come through sound policies and procedures followed by good training; the last must come through a caring and engaged leader who is genuinely motivated and fully resolved to grow and develop people under his command. Commanders who take great pride in their ability and track record at the success of the professional growth and development of their people are true servant leaders and are extremely successful Commanders with very effective work units.

The world today has evolved to a state of almost total transparency as it relates to the political, economic, and cultural winds of globalization. The unique combination of media, Internet utilities, and other technologies has closed distance and connected people like no other time in human history. Issues, events, and incidents are discovered, analyzed, interpreted, discussed, and broadcast throughout the world at lightning speed. An argument begins based upon and rooted in the objective or subjective method and manner information is processed and viewed due to subjective rhetoric and ideology. Credibility and reputations are attacked or bolstered, while propositions and hypothesis are designed and promoted as a result of passionate philosophy, ulterior motives, or idiosyncratic ideals.

In this environment, the frailties and strengths of the human condition are seen in action in the middle of life's theater, thus resulting from any particular person at any particular time; each character that shapes their thoughts may translate that into conduct and behavior, good or bad, and disseminate that. In these terms, history has shown and the future will sustain three separate characteristics of human traits as outlined at the end of chapter one.

The key is having the faith, fortitude, self-confidence, and courage to put others first and trust the fact that the more one does for others, the more one will help himself in the end. From job performance to job results, a servant leader builds teams that succeed every time. And from that success comes motivation and dedication toward the job, organization, and purpose. Such devotion develops a natural loyalty, appreciation, and respect for the Commander. Subordinates know, deep inside, you helped to get them where they are, to that success-summit, and they recognize the importance of their relationship with and to you.

Something that has really helped me throughout the years is my sincere ability to take joy from others that have been successful. This is a huge advantage for one to evolve into a real servant leader that will advance one's skills as a Commander. When one becomes truly happy for others instead of envious or jealous, he will have reached a huge leadership milestone, one that builds self-confidence from real-selflessness that will be seen, absorbed, and digested by everyone. This reputation will create and sustain the foundation to build your influence and persuasive abilities that are critical components to competent and effective leadership.

I have had supervisors that, for some unknown reason, could not share in the delight of others' successes. This disposition cultivated adverse situations. It is absolutely essential that a Commander take pride and exhibit sincere joy when those under her change do well or are successful. If she can learn to not only sincerely feel that joy, but openly demonstrate her joy, her relational currency will grow exponentially.

Another trait of a true servant-leader is one who takes pride, endorses, and does all he or she can do to help subordinates better themselves. From being promoted up the chain, transferred to a sought after position or seeking a better position or employment opportunity elsewhere. Often, this attitude requires the leader suffer the loss of an experienced employee and feel an adverse impact from more work due to their good fortune. However, when a leader embraces the notion of true joy in their "betterment" and they know it then those under his or her command will be open and tell of their plans and coming opportunities and share information when they apply for advancement or change. Moreover, these employees will work harder because the spirit of worth the leader demonstrates toward them will infectious throughout the work unit to motivate others. I remember as a task force commander, just when I would get an agent trained and have them where they needed to be an opportunity would occur for advancement. I would work to get them promoted and start with another "rookie" agent, but that rookie agent saw and knew what would happen in their future if they did their part. That paid me huge dividends.

Moreover, successful people often become more successful and the more successful one's people, the more successful one becomes; remember, the Commander bears the ultimate responsibility when things go bad and when things go good. The difference in leadership between a successful and non-successful leader comes when things go good – the leader gives all the credit – and when things go bad – the leader takes all the responsibility; the leader never excuses or blames others. He holds accountable, yet also ameliorates. This recipe will lead to exemplary trust and loyalty from people under his charge.

In July 2010, the University of Louisville produced an exploratory study on "Idea Leadership Behavior" by surveying 126 police managers from 23 states regarding ranking the importance of leadership characteristics based upon police officers perspectives to create a "typology" of preferred leadership styles. Viviana Andreescu and Gennaro F. Vito, the study's authors, found that police managers who participated in the research felt that ideal leaders should primarily be able to reconcile conflicting demands and reduce disorder in the system. Leaders should be persuasive, convincing, and able to set the vision for the organization. Leaders should clearly define their roles and subordinates responsibilities, set examples, and respond to followers' expectations. Their conclusion? Leaders should take care of their people and integrate them into to the organization while promoting wellbeing.

What's more, in 2011 an article titled "Emphasizing the Servant in Public Service: The Opinions of Police Managers" in the publication "Policing – An International Journal of Police Strategies and Management" Gennaro F. Vito, Geetha Suresh, and George E. Richards revealed findings suggesting that police managers strongly preferred the servant leadership style, and erred to often reject the creeds of both the "autocratic command and control" and the "hands off-detached" style of laissez-faire leadership.

I found a perfect assessment of a servant leader hidden within the pages of an old 1949 Snowdon-Douglass yearly Sunday school lesson book I found on the shelves of a thrift store; part of it read: "Successful people have themselves well in hand and where there is no inner conflict there is abundant evidence of peace and assurance, knowing where they stand, why and how they stand they know where they are and the direction where they arc headed. They walk with confidence because they are sure of themselves and their position." When you are self-confident but not self-absorbed you have the power and ability to gain the influence to do anything, the key is retaining the self-discipline to fight ego and keep the fine balance between self-confidence/self-esteem and selfishness and pride. The highest and best way to fight the frailties of the human condition that coxes and seduces us into its natural trap is to struggle everyday being aware and knowing that you play devil's advocate with yourself on every motive, objectively evaluate your thoughts and behaviors through an empathic prism narrowly tailored toward the good of the organization and those under your command then you must seek feedback from those around you to ensure an environment of trust, transparency and openness. This formula will create a culture of honest and candid communications and enhanced job performance and results. This difficult recipe cannot be brought together, prepared and place on the workplace table without the mindset of humility blended into the personal and professional self-confidence by the commander. This leadership perspective and preferred nature of conduct was captured in words best by the author C.S. Lewis who once said, "Humility is not thinking less of yourself, its thinking of yourself less"

James M. Kouzes and Barry Z. Posners' research from Leadership Challenge model in 2002, and a later study by Vito and Higgins at the University of Louisville, provided findings that support the model as being valid for understanding leadership capabilities among law enforcement officers and I believe many other occupations.

They determined five important practices:

1. **Model the way:** Set the example.

2. **Inspire:** Share vision.

3. **Challenge the process:** Confront the status quo.

4. **Enable others:** Nurture and empower.

5. **Encourage the Heart:** Recognize accomplishments.

Values lie at the heart of "Model the way." Values are significant because they influence how leaders respond to others. Further, added values create passion, motivate, and inspire others. They underline the fact the significance oriented beliefs create genuine leaders. They also find that "modeling is ultimately tied to competency."

"Inspire" finds leaders aligning their actions with shared values, building consensuses, teaching, storytelling, and kindling values by personal example.

"Challenge the process" deals with how leaders envision the future, how they articulate their vision to inspire their followers. This means listening to their people and the desires of their people. Leaders always challenge the process in order to become better.

"Enable others" finds leaders enlisting others in a common vision by appealing to their shared aspirations. Seeking to move follows to action will improve organizational performance. Leaders seek to seize the initiative, to make the organization more effective and efficient.

Lastly, "Encourage the heart" impels leaders to seek innovative, change-centric ways to grow and improve those who they command, to experiment and take risk. Leaders encourage followers to take small steps, achieve small wins that generate enthusiasm and support. When followers take risks to move the organization forward, the leader never punishes or chastises because they know it would destroy initiative.

These leaders look at making mistakes as learning. Leaders foster collaboration and create climates of trust through which tasks are invariably completed. They also noted: "The most effective leaders are servant leaders who assume their role and responsibilities for the purpose of meeting the needs of others."

They also noted that a leader who gives up their power to their followers ultimately increases their own power. These leaders inspire confidence and competence, they celebrate the accomplishments of their followers, and they focus on high standards, always holding people accountable.

Anthony Batts, Sean Michael Smoot, and Ellen Scrivner in, "Police Leadership Challenges in a Changing World" from Harvard and The National Institute of Justice's 2012 perspectives in policing does an excellent job of warning us: "In many police departments, little or no investment is made in training first-line supervisors in the art and methods of mentorship or coaching. Successful organizational leadership in an agency focused on community-oriented or problem solving policing must incorporate a break from complacent first-line supervision and officer evaluation processes that measure job performance based on activity statistics or ticket quotas. Instead, a real investment must be made in training for supervisors that emphasis guidance through mentoring, leadership through instruction, education, logic and persuasion are the "power tools" of contemporary police leadership...not "do as I say"...and they are consistent with the needs of the new generation of contemporary employees."

Next, I need to address commander's responsibilities to prevent, mitigate, and reduce occupational stress. Stress is a huge issue in today's workplace; there is tremendous evidence available that shows that organizational stress can be devastating to an individual and destroy the effectiveness of a work unit.

Historically, we have thought about stress as a result of the nature of police work, high-speed chases, observation of violent crime scenes, terrible trauma and death in accidents, and other daily dangers. These and other typical duties are sure measures that can cause stress. A large amount of information today centers upon a more constant, regular and lasting internal stress that may be worse than all the traditional sources of external stress.

Jeanne B. Stinchcomb, in her July 2004 Article in "Police Practice and Research" stated it well: "Chronic sources of organizationally in-duced stress that have the capacity for taking a far greater toll on long term health and well-being of police personnel. From unclear expec-tations to inadequate communications, insufficient rewards, and au-tocratic management practices." Stinchcomb went on to say: "Stress is more likely to be involved in the helping professions because of both the nature of such work and the nature of stress itself. In terms of work, this means that the less control employees have over what they are expected to do and the outcome of their efforts, the more stress they are likely to experience." Stinchcomb pointed out that the traditional top down management of police organizations has been identified as a common source of stress. She goes on the say: "those agencies have viewed stress as an individual disorder rather than an organizational dysfunction." Transformational leaders through their dedication to servant-hood characteristics and participative management styles can help reduce oc-cupational stressors within the context of the workplace.

Most importantly, I need to provide the key to a servant leader's abil-ity to be seen as sincere, empathetic, trustworthy, and effective. This key rests in the ability of the leader to "adopt" others problems. The strategy of "problem adoption" is when the leader makes their subordi-nates problem as theirs, thus not only taking ownership, but also work-ing through the issues just like the very problem belonged to the them in the beginning. This iskey because if you own it, you will do everything in your power to fix it and those who had the problem mitigated or fixed will know your sacrifice and effort.

Finally, as the Commander, you inherit many responsibilities that vary in different levels of priority. One of the very top priorities is your professional obligation in a private context with your employees during the good and bad times. From hospital visits to funerals, a wedding to a baby's birth, all of these times are very important and emotional events where your employee doesn't need to worry about work and needs to know those in authority care. Never miss these events whether joyful or tragic; your presence and support will be heartfelt and comforting to your employee and their family members. Moreover, it's the fitting and proper way to be. Your people need the recognition and support of the "boss" so that they know and understand the work place is second, that they are first in these rare but life changing events.

Many times I was tired, under pressure with other issues, or just wanted my time off; I knew sending flowers or a card was nice, but I needed to get in the car, show up, and be there for my employee. It built relational currency and was the right thing to do in my attempt to be a servant-leader. You never get involved in people's personal business unless it affects their professional obligations as an employee. However, there is a responsibility to support and encourage them in and at certain times.

Chapter Four:
"THE BURDEN OF COMMUNICATION"

"The art of communication is the language of leadership."
-- James Humes

Dr. Peter F. Drucker, famed management expert, once said: "Communication is perception, is expectation, and makes demands... communication and information are different and indeed largely opposite yet interdependent."

In Plato's "Phaedo," one of the earliest extant treatises on rhetoric, Socrates points out that one must converse with others in terms of those others' own experiences. Percept and concept are not separate.

I have a habit of using a years-old phrase in my conversations with people. It goes something like this, "Do you see what I'm saying." I believe its origins to be original because I can't remember any place or time I picked it up from anyone else. My belief remains that the saying is a product of my deep desire for people to understand me. In very basic, fundamental, and elementary terms to "see" something is to "understand" something. We want people to understand us, and as Commanders in influential positions that require leadership, this idea is one of the most important. At the end of the day great communication is about being able to relay a message that others understand.

Like so many others who write about communication, I have found one needs to plan and make effort to ensure he keeps his content simple, creditable, consistent, and meaningful. Simplicity is the rule. Why? Because the reduction of effort lowers the level-knowledge quotient required to catch, process, and understand the message received and sent. Simplicity guarantees the best chance for the broadest audience to comprehend and understand information in the shortest time.

For the purposes of total comprehension, and to promote a workable understanding, let's look at Merriam-Webster's definition of "context."

1. The parts of discourse – the capacity of orderly thought, rationality, and the verbal exchange of ideas especially conversation – that surround a word or passage and can cast light on its meaning.

2. The interrelated conditions in which something exists or occurs: its environment or setting.

The first definition leads toward the conversational use of words and their meanings within any particular manner and method used; the second tends to describe and articulate the nature of the atmosphere, terrain, landscape, and geography of the territory that the path or road one has chosen to travel. It also deals with the spatial-temporal, circumstantial, and conditional natures that influence the situations or issues afoot.

Context not only promotes understanding and prepares the ground ahead for the cultivation of those vital communicable seeds to take root and grow, but enhances the circumstances for success and mitigates failure-risk when interacting with others both verbally and non-verbally. It all boils down to trust. For communication to be understood, it must be trusted.

Credibility is the central ingredient of trust. Never lie; never say you know when you don't know. There is wisdom, not weakness, in admitting you don't know about any particular item, idea, or method. Faking in order to sustain the appearance and perceptions of trustworthiness communication conveyance paves a slippery, winding road that most often terminates in a dead end.

Inherently, as humans, we feel weak, inferior, or insecure when we're unable to answer questions, especially simple ones we know we must or are required to know. Oftentimes, in these situations, we feel, perhaps, we must embellish, bend the truth, "BS" even. Thus, we have a tendency to take the path of deception rather than truth.

Dr. Harry W. Frankfurt illustrated this phenomenon well: "Bullshit is unavoidable whenever circumstances require someone to talk without knowing what they are talking about. Thus, the production of bullshit is stimulated whenever a person's obligations or opportunities to speak about some topic exceed their knowledge of the facts that are relevant to that topic." Credibility is an essential component to able communication and effective command. One can never sacrifice his credibility, ruin his reputation, by not being responsible and diligent in his communications to others. He must be confident, knowledgeable, and then, importantly, uniform in that confidence and knowledge within his communication.

Consistency provides stability, builds the ability to follow the meaning, vision, and expectation of communication. It promotes adaptability that forges calm transitions and demonstrates one's command over the message and competence in their subject matter. People are naturally more comfortable with consistency. Meaningfulness is a product of purpose and is necessary to set goals, identify objectives, gauge performances and promote "buy in."

In communications, so much begins with how we start: our contact, our content, and our contexts are huge factors in the process that begins with communication and ends at understanding. How we approach others, what we show others through our conduct, our behavior, and our action looms huge in forming those so-important first impressions, entities that others use as the inaugurals of attention based involvement, or lack of depending on the circumstance. Thus, we must ensure we plan ahead and set the stage to embrace the opportunity to gain interest and promote trust in the establishment of an exemplary "emotional contact environment;" seize the moment in our favor. Be heard and understood; promote feedback. First impressions are always important; they can – and often do – influence our opinions, shape our beliefs, and drive our decision-making. They are the very mold in which our mindsets are formed. What we see in others, hear from others and, believe in others – in the context of our first meetings – all claim tremendous influence upon us and the way we view them.

First impressions provide the initial window of opportunity to foster trust and create relationships. Sound relationships drive communications in positive ways and promote good results. Accurate perceptions and first impressions contain and obtain many factors. Research suggests that the space between individuals at the time of meeting, facial expressions exposed upon first contact, and body language and eye movement correlated to original meeting are just some of the major sources of non-verbal signals that individuals interpret in different ways during the first-impression.

Besides body language, other factors such as personal demeanor, mannerisms, dress, and general appearance also blend into one's evaluations and judgments of others. These physical yet non-verbal components of communication are tremendously important in the assessment and evaluation process; as an effective leader, plan prior to any communication to ensure and stack the odds in your favor. Make sure you endeavor to be heard and understood by others in a meaningful fashion. But, most importantly in this context, remember this: "How you say something and when you say something means everything." It doesn't take any additional effort to be nice to people; form words carefully; craft sentences elegantly; and intone inflections empathetically.

Again, as I have stated in earlier chapters, context is paramount in every aspect, especially in one's efforts to communicate effectively. Providing context upfront establishes the importance and value of the information. Moreover, it ties into why the information is relevant for them particularly and to them particularly. This makes your information matter to them, and that's the goal, right? Capture attention, interest, and thought and you will capture anyone.

We all have experienced good waiters and waitresses and bad waiters and waitresses. We have experienced the one who takes the time to smile, make eye contact, and, tactfully, convey story relating to the different menu items or courses based on their perceived notions of us. Those service professionals capture our attention, promote our interest, and influence our decisions based upon their explanations of entree content with the preoperational context unique to their restaurant. They know their stuff. These efforts usually pay dividends in large tips and, from time to time, and more often than not, interesting and engaging communications exchanges.

Effective communication is an end that begins with a journey that requires planning, thoughtful assessment, and structured expression, alongside articulate gestures, urbane conduct, and tactful appearance rooted in sincerity and genuine care and concern for the issues that affect all parties. One must use the terms discussed in the burden of self-awareness to promote his abilities as a great communicator.

However, it's not simply the context that's important, but also the content. The message, or content, is what truly captures one's interest and develops "buy-in" about the conversation and ongoing dialogue. Careful consideration of the components of the message and how will such a message will be received must be weighed and evaluated within the terms of how such materials may affect the individual concerned and with what degree of change such may influence.

Being empathetic toward others' feelings and factoring that empathy into the way one designs her content and deliver her message is tremendously important in the sustaining interest and promotional "buy-in" of the subject of her efforts. This, blended with context, is where one blends everything together in a palatable way, one through which information can be digested in calm, thoughtful, and deliberate manners. The arena of operation is built through one's efforts to place everything in a fair, logical, and understandable context.

I like to use an age old method, one tried by history and proven through rhetoric to be of great utility in the entire communication process. It is the rhetorical triangle, a representational allegory for how the trilateral relationship between Pathos, Ethos, and Logos informs, builds, and elicits communication.

First, Pathos, that all-important ability to capture, harness, and use one's emotions to reflect and assess issues afoot, forms the basis of the pyramid. Pathos spurs feelings and beliefs inside one's mind and body, feelings and beliefs that make one accept, reject, or thirst for more. The abilities to stir emotions and fuel spirits are tremendously important in the quest to persuade or influence others.

Next, Ethos, the thought process illuminated by another through reputation, information, or observation that gives someone credibility and promotes trust, forms the gut of the pyramid. The implied sense of veracity on one's behalf, and in what she says and does, is integral to the way others perceive her propensity to and of trustworthiness and honor. It is not just what she says and how she says it, but of also the perception of who she is and what she represents that is remarkably important and exceedingly meaningful.

Then, Logos, that reasonable, logical and common sense demonstration of what one is trying to convey, to have others comprehend and understand, forms the pinnacle of the pyramid. Logos must be delivered in a basic and fundamental way through simple illustration and descriptive narrative. One wants the individual he is talking with to "see what he's saying" through his means of articulation and examples driven articulation. One must "paint the picture" through experiential anecdote and relative and relatable analogies.

Lastly, the rhetorical triangle's three components must be delivered at the right place and time. Kairos – the right timing for the message – becomes tremendously important. This timing goes right to the heart of "context" as well. There are times where one must improve her chances for good communication by waiting; there are times she must seize the opportunity by moving at lightning speed. Nonetheless, all must be based upon and rooted in the totality of the facts and circumstances of every particular situation and how such effects everyone involved.

This is the bottom line: when one looks at communication through the prism of "contact, content, and context" and applies an empathic angle of view, in combination with the planning and use of the rhetorical triangle, he will vastly improve his chances and abilities to communicate with efficacy.

For years, I had a sign glued to the office wall on a plastic placard. It hung above my door and only I could see it. In big, red capital letters it read, "LISTEN." Every day it reminded me of the basics when I looked up from my desk and toward my door when someone entered to see me. I did this out of necessity because I knew I was *not* a good listener and the sign reminded me of the huge obligation and of the commanding necessity of listening-improvement. Of course I was passionate; I was quite the deft talker and could "out-talk" the best, promote my own theories and postulations, and express my opinions with great regularity and dominance. However, that skillset didn't come close to carrying the relational cachet that deliberate and thoughtful listening did, and in every situation, not just some.

There are two types of listening patterns: Active and Passive. Active listeners aggressively listen and absorb information with great attention in order to apply what they have learned sometimes immediately. Passive listeners listen to others with diminished degrees of interest and attention, but still retain, apply, or use gathered information actively, however later and in differing degrees operation. They often use knowledge garnered in this fashion to build upon their learning, personal growth, and professional development in the long term.

I learned early how tremendously important listening was, not only for me to process and understand important information to increase my personal competence, but how tremendously important it was in its influence of others who were so intent upon speaking and being heard. I learned that when I aggressively listened to others not only did it help me, but it also helped them. I began to understand the importance of conveying importance through my listening to them, of my allowing them to be important, well received, and, most importantly, understood.

Good communication will always rest upon and rely on a two way process where the sender and the receiver are joined together through interest, attention, thoughtful consideration, and feedback. Listening is first and foremost the capstone in the communication arch.

Moreover, study after study has demonstrated that nonverbal dominion over the verbal side of communications often produces desired results. Aggressive listening produces sincere and credible nonverbal patterns that produce and build trust. Trust is essential in all communications and the application of goals and objectives. My sign reminded me of this, and helped sustain my behavior toward such difficult ends in order to cultivate discipline within myself to listen and empower.

Communication is the means to express ideas and provide arguments that focus upon finding truth and providing solutions to ever evolving issues in any organization. The ability to communicate ideas and arguments rests upon and is incumbent on the planning, design, implementation, and management of a leader's communiqué repertoire. Communication is the glue that holds organizations together, creates and sustains relationships, and promotes performance. Communication is an essential skill of a leader; it is one that must be excellent and robust, one that must cultivate the great communicator into the great leader. The ability to articulate, describe purpose, and cast vision toward achieving meaningful and important purposes can only occur and exude from a leader who knows how to correctly communicate and one who understands the value and priority placed upon the time devoted toward it. The leader who first identifies all stakeholders, then crafts careful and well thought out messages directed and routed based upon relationships, roles, and responsibilities, will be successful.

Ensure, in the process of identifying stakeholders, that one never leaves anyone out. Forgetting any individual that should have been included in the communication process is the functional equivalent of telling them they are not important. When one stops and takes time to identify all internal and external stakeholders, he greatly reduces the chances of leaving one of those stakeholders out. Making a habit of this process is well worth the exertion involved; the more labor involved the greater the ability to limit the risk in exigent, ad hoc, or emotion prone instances of communications alienation, which, in the long run, may adversely affect those one may need later in his operations and development.

Many find it difficult to forget and forgive when they are hurt personally, professionally or, most of the time, both; they don't enjoy being left out, forgotten, or rebutted. Thinking about one's stakeholders and how to relate and intertwine relevant issues is tremendously important. Do not forget to also consider, in this same context, authority, jurisdiction, and the hierarchy involved with each stakeholder and how it relates to the reasons for communication, purpose of the message, need to know, and right to know. Always lean toward global and complete inclusion of all stakeholders when appropriate and feasible. When the nature of the communication and facts involved require limiting dissemination, develop a plan to deal with each stakeholder in delayed explanation – explanation provided at a different, more feasible time – or damage control. The key is being proactive in one's ability to consider, being proactive in his thoughtfulness and fairness toward all stakeholders, and proactive in his ability to maintain any and all individual respect.

Everyone wants to be important and valuable in life; people seek and desire to be recognized and be given attention. The initial step in all communications resides in the knowledge to recognize this human need and to demonstrate the acumen to satisfy this need and create interest. It is always necessary to capture one's attention, to gain his interest, and to promote his empowerment through acute and intentioned listening, something that will more often than not translate into understanding.

But achieving that understanding doesn't mean just capturing one's attention.

One wants and needs another's interest, not just his attention. Interest opens the proverbial communication door and provides both momentum and command; the difference between attention and interest is one's motives or bent toward recognizing the potential benefit for his other in the message. If he can create an idea or cast a shadow of benefit over the other that will give him their attention and invest their interest in what he says. The position he establishes provides the best opportunity to be heard and the optimum luxury to be understood.

This illustrates why it is so important at the onset to cultivate interest and capture attention. Interest is fostered when a careful and intentional plan is in made and stellar communication skills are used alongside a favorable message; importance is meaningful to the receiver's condition and/or situation. In other words, any message expressed that contains relevant information has a high probability to affect the receiver. This demonstrates why one must carefully design all communication for content, context, and intent in a meaningful fashion. The bottom line is this: "Produce the ability to make yourself interesting and understood."

But where does it all begin? How does worthwhile and engaging communication start?

It all begins with contact. Make a rule to contact and have a conversation with people when you do not need anything. Demonstrate that you contact people because you value their input, opinions, and ideas, not just what they can do for you. This will go a long way in giving you a certain communicational credibility among those in your network. This is a huge step in the development of relational currency development. Such builds respect, trust, and credibility.

In any normative context, in any normal circumstances, one can be strong, possess authority, exercise influence, and promote persuasion far more efficiently and effectively when she is nice to people. Often, what she says does not have as much impact as how she says it; such can and does shape conversation and mold results of the communications efficacy. Being calm, respectful, cordial, conscientious, and pleasant is of tremendous benefit to further one's communication efforts. It is also labor intensive, so be prepared; she must continuously work to recognize her intention, converse cordially, and contentiously follow up by remembering each individual and their interests and concerns.

Another important key in effective communication is patience; imperative relational cultivation, patience in aggressive listening pays copious dividends when practiced properly. When fact-finding is required, patience should cultivate a deliberately skeptical assessment carefully evaluating the totality of facts and circumstances. The process should progress from general to specific with objective, thorough, and thoughtful analysis. Always welcome the opportunity to explain the process, the necessary elements required, and how those elements are incorporated into the overall base conclusion for accurate and understandable support. Then listen aggressively to chart the next course. Often times, one of the most important advantages in communication is the ability to form and design the next question. Patient listening fuels this notion and improves each question's content and result.

In his book, "It's Your Ship," Captain Michael Abrashoff explains that individuals are far more likely to speak aggressively than to listen aggressively. Abrashoff states that when he decided to dedicate himself to be an intentional listener, it changed him and his crew entirely. He was observant and tuned in to his crew, their needs, and, in order to change, his own needs.

Consequently, being observant stands as another linchpin in the effectiveness of the communication process. We all know and understand a huge portion of our communication is non-verbal, is body language. Demeanor, mood, and attitude combine with patterns of conduct, behavior, and reactionary facial expressions and speak volumes without word or sentence.

These types of internal – and sometimes external – self-observations provide clues to a ours and others' attitudes and abilities for understanding and comprehension. Moreover, such provide credible forecasts of one's trust endorsements versus one's skeptical assessments for change. Most important information and feedback is garnered from listening and observing the non-verbal.

If one gains interest, secures trust, builds relationships, sustains credibility, listens to feedback, uses others' ideas and solutions, and then factors everyone into his communication agenda, gives them credit, and recognizes effort, he will invariably develop a culture of worthwhile information dissemination, one where subordinates will tell him what he needs to know versus what he wants to hear; this type of atmosphere continually keeps one in a state of situational awareness within his organization. This is a tremendously necessary requirement for a strong leader and proficient manager. Neither he nor his boss must ever be surprised. More often than not, one might better deal with circumstances if he is made adequately aware of about them and has the benefit of time-allotment to conduct damage control; it's the surprise issues that create chaos, that spiral situations and organizations out of control.

We live in a world where work place and home run at lightning speed; we are busy people. In order to communicate well, we have to first realize the need of, and second, take the time and effort to assess and mend those needs. Factor in the barriers of today's communications – the Internet, continuous data streams, foci on materials instead of relationship, etc – and it's a wonder we even communicate at all. But doesn't the Internet facilitate communication? Doesn't widely accessible data confer communication between interested parties? Doesn't material focused endeavor push the need of effective communication amongst governments, industries, and peoples? Perhaps; perhaps not.

I would argue that those types of things have made other things more difficult. An example would be cell phones and how one call at the right time, in the right place, in the middle of our conversation, if answered thrusts the whole communications loop into a tailspin. Or maybe the culprit is a "flaming arrow" e-mail that "thumps" on your desk at four o'clock on Friday with a due date of Monday morning.

Today's world, filled with so much interference and activity, handicaps one's ability to listen without a fight, to devote himself wholly to the listening process, to include those very important non-verbal's so previously discussed. Most experts say that over 75 percent of human communication is non-verbal; consequently, why would one ever decide to carry on an important conversation by email? One can't see that frown, hear that screech, or feel that nervous perspiration over a computer monitor. I have found it far more rewarding and valuable to, as much as possible, speak to and communicate with one face to face. Furthermore, as social creatures that require social interaction and dialogue, such interactivity builds upon the all-important foundation of relationship. Time devoted to people is attention devoted to people, attention devoted to people is credibility devoted to accurate communications.

I would further argue that modern technologies often times impede our ability to listen effectively as well. We only listen well when we make it a priority to listen well. My old friend Romie Waters, a great communicator, once told me: "God gave you two ears and one mouth and a lot of folks ain't realized it yet". Use those ears and that mouth to aggressively listen, to maintain that loop of effectiveness and efficiency.

Communication takes planning and preparation, careful and deliberate engagement, and persistent follow up. "It ain't what you know... it's who you know;" relationships are the currency for life interactions and organizational success. Everything is based upon and rooted in relationships, thus our ability to build, sustain, and enhance relationships is critical toward any goal, objective, or purpose we want to achieve.

Relationships drive our ability to get things done, receive important tangible or intangible materials, capture interest, attention, and respect, or become meaningful and important to any endeavor or organizational advancement. And relationships require motivation.

Great leaders become "relational engineers" dedicated to the constant and ongoing building and sustaining of internal and external relationships in and around the organization.

A true catalyst for the injury to and original death of motivation is the personal grievances one feels when he perceives or believes he has been ignored, left out, or forgotten. This state of self-worthlessness occurs when the leader fails to properly notify and communicate regular issues within the organization. A leader's people will first take it personal and then immediately speak of failure, its anticipated consequences, and the predictions of its results. The pattern and consistent statement of opinion arises that will solidify this into solid fact: "everybody else knows about what's going on in this organization but us."

Now the die is cast and the perception becomes reality. The importance of the continuing fight against the incessant and monumental burden to communicate shows its face again. The leader must command the environment and mold the atmosphere into a state where communication becomes priority and systems and networks are in place, active, and ongoing that sustain this ideal every day, every week, every year. Implementation of functioning structures and networks to provide, assess, and promote outreach to those under one's charge will alleviate problems, elevate motivation, and enhance performance.

The drama of human emotions and feelings can truly be touched with the need or right to be privy to the information. This component can, and mostly will, be taken personally if not followed. This is why it is so critical to follow the rule of Roles, of Responsibilities, and of Relationships in the communication routes and courses.

It is difficult for one to cry foul on the issue of fairness if the issue is beyond their role or responsibility within the scope of their duties within the organization. A huge part of this strategy is never allowing relationships to drive or steer one's routes and determine the people contacted; stick to necessary responsibility. If one designs and disciplines himself to the 3R's – Roles, Responsibilities, and Relationships – she will prevent many problems by adequately protecting the feelings of others.

The central factor in the planning, design, implementation, and management of any communication structure or system is it creates a situation where if the people do not get the information it is their fault. Paramount to this theory of communication outreach and delivery is the culture of redundancy. Redundancy creates habit, promotes, recall and institutionalizes the systems and networks one designs, implements, and manages.

When I talk about redundancy in these terms, I mean that one's process is completed time and time again in a consistent and predictable fashion. Situational briefings, regularly scheduled updates, and staff meetings can be the forums for the cultivation of redundancy. Nothing, however, can substitute for "face-time" and regular follow up for feedback. This takes thought and time; it is a labor-intensive process within the communication matrix that stems from the application of message content and context that ultimately aids others in joining the leader in his vision for not only himself, but also his organization and, most importantly, his subordinates.

Empathy is another important component in being able to help others; it is tremendously important for people to see the empathetic outreach at the beginning of any conversation or interaction between you and them. Dr. Heilman, in a 1972 study, found that there are three main characteristics in the ability for one to empathize with another.

1. The ability to accurately perceive the content of another's message.

2. The ability to give attention to the emotional components and the unexpressed core meanings of any particular message.

3. The ability to maintain an "as if" quality, as self-sacrificing perspective.

For one to truly demonstrate he is an empathetic listener, he must be sensitive to the content, feelings, and underlying message being conveyed and/or expressed to others. He must maintain an open mind and attempt to see the frame of reference held by the other party. He must withhold evaluations and judgments while maintaining attention and sustaining interest in others' point of view. He must factor empathetic responses into his interchanges, while focusing upon content and context; finally, he must be conscientious and understanding toward resistance, toward inappropriate responses, toward mislead beliefs, and toward inaccurate interpretations and perceptions. His depth of relationship with the other party will serve as measure toward the levels of openness or resistance he will experience. The better the relationship, the better the opportunities for receiving, processing, and understanding the information communicated. Comprehension and acceptance is the ultimate goal in one's responsibility to cast vision and guide and direct conduct and behavior.

Remember, emotion plays a huge part in the communication loop and is critical, in the beginning, in how a message is sought, received, and interpreted. When one keeps her people informed, subordinates feel they are a part of the bigger team; they develop ownership that generates care and concern regarding outcomes. How can one see purpose and experience meaningful conditions at work if they are kept in the shadows? The answer: they can't.

Moreover, the attention from and benefits of exemplary communication inventory and outreach produces an outstanding situational environment for dealing with issues proactively and arbitrating informed decisions that produce desired results.

It is an absolute burden to maintain and sustain good communication. Moreover, good communication will not occur unless one makes it an absolute priority. Priorities become priorities only when leaders place emphases upon their importance, and then hold everyone accountable inside a zero tolerance sphere for failure. Communication is the cornerstone for building relationships, preventing problems, and casting vision for the future.

I have always found it regrettable that we, in general, have not and do not make communication the priority it needs to be. I believe the primary reason for our failure to place such a high premium upon communication is the state of our affairs in combination with the labor intensive process stellar communication demands. Further, our modern culture – of which I wrote about earlier – brings different mediums of communication with different paths and manners. The mobility of smart phones provides every-second access to a wide range of mediums with no one person using the same means of operation. These cell phones interrupt meals, meetings and conversations, and provide instantaneous texting and email that becomes analogous to flaming arrows landing in a dry forest; they rush, detract, and impede the skill to promote good communications through an effective and, in ways, admiring fire-sail. However, don't misunderstand: smart phones and other technologies can be and are used to great benefit in many thoughtful strategies within communication, but usually when they remain the secondary and not the primary means for communicating in the workplace, especially as a leader.

I remember a friend of mine, Rusty Andrews, a deputy director in the GBI, who regularly emailed all the agents under his charge as information outreach to promote good communication, kill rumors, and welcome ideas and feedback regarding pending issues. This email strategy was not only received well, but became the standard first-step in launching face-to-face meetings. Rumors lead to infections of mistaken beliefs that spread exponentially across the work unit landscape and require proactive treatment before the symptoms occur and result in communication sickness.

At the Evans County Sheriff's Office, we created a LISTSERV of email addresses that included all law enforcement in the county; it was designed to provide state of the art communication. All local, state and federal agencies received a daily email titled, "E-Roll Call'" this email provided a vetted list of all Sheriff's Office and city police calls from the night prior. Thus, every officer knew what had gone on the night before and knew what each was doing. Further, officers were able to "connect the dots" regarding crime, order maintenance issues and events, dispel rumors, and possess a proactive situational awareness. These officers were also safer and far more effective and efficient at their jobs. A positive unintended consequence is their use of past e-mails on their phones to revisit to "connect the dots" or "build cause" to corroborate earlier issues to investigate new ones.

This system was very successful for three reasons. First, it provided accurate and real-time information to everyone. Second, it provided a meaningful purpose toward work. Third, it provided officers leadership-catered information. In essence, this type of efficiency is what all communication system should at least attempt to achieve.

The inside story here is one of leadership, challenging the status quo, adapting to change, and innovating. The overwhelming majority of police and sheriff's offices in our country do not have full time intelligence analysts. This is someone who will watch, identify, and correlate crime occurrences and patterns within a geographical context. Further, analysts work to gather criminal intelligence information, vet for accuracy and relevancy, and then store and disseminate it to officers for action. Analysts constantly watch open source social media and the web for leads and clues to criminal acts or misconducts. The key to an analyst position is to discover treats ahead of time, develop actions to mitigate those treats and as a result prevent crime from ever occurring in the first place. This strategy of proactively preventing, disrupting, eliminating, and reducing crime makes a law enforcement agency far more effective and efficient, and makes everyone safer and secure.

The reason is that much more emphasis is placed upon a sworn officer to do regular police work, fill the shift, cover the calls for service. A sworn officer is seen as the best bang for the buck through their utility in an agency's responsibilities, but in the context of 21st century, changes in technologies, communications, and cultures does not exalt the networks, systems, and structures of the means and methods we communicate create opportunity to use data and information more effective and efficiency compared to routine patrol where we ride and look? This is the tradition and how it has always been done.

The Sheriff of Evans County, Randall Tippins, had over 30 years of experience in law enforcement and had a reputation for being an industrious and astute investigator; moreover, he was passionate. Tippins knew the importance of communication, the conveyance of intelligence information, and how, over many years, this knowledge had been so meaningful toward his successes in important cases and everyday policing. Tippins also strived to develop and grow his competency in the intelligence field to insure he could seize the initiative in the evaluations of new technologies without ever coming close to invading another's privacy rights.

Thus, Tippins made the decision to challenge the status quo and the norm by hiring a sworn officer, Bryant Jones, in a non-sworn position; Further, Tippins trained Bryant as a full time crime and intelligence analyst. Tippins' vision was to promote exemplary communication, coordination, and drive on and within operations data versus hunches and history. In the end, the endeavor was successful, and in the end Tippins created a tremendously beneficial program that has been selected as a national best practice by the United States Bureau of Justice Assistance, the subject of many national publications and lectures at the International Association of Chiefs of Police and national Sheriff's association.

Tippins took the risk and chose his course because he absolutely knew the value of communication in today's world. As a result, Tippins, through his Intelligence Led Policing program starting with Jones' "buy in" and performance theory, and ending with the lion heart centurions who risk their lives every day, had significantly reduced crime and disorder in Evans County. And it was all based upon and firmly rooted in the art and science of modern communication. Commanders and managers must be able to make operations perform well as a result of their leadership skills; communication promotes exemplary performance at all levels.

I started policing in 1977; all I had back then was a four-channel, limited range Motorola radio; I had to know the location of various pay phones in our county. Today we have smart phones with cell service, texting, and email. We have radios with different bands and hundreds of channels that use digital systems with no range limits. I can make an argument that although the technology improvements have enhanced and vastly improved the ability and opportunity for some communication, and in other instances have degraded the quality of our communications.

It is so important we understand these modern technologies and how they relate to good communication philosophies and skills. Technologies are tools and the basic rules of communications still apply. Technologies must not conflict with our human nature, laws, community standards, ethics, and expected conducts and behaviors. Remember, in the 21st century, perception is reality, and we must remain sensitive to the images we portray toward others. In this century, tolerance and objectivity are required, subjective virtues in their application and evaluation by different peoples, groups, or organizations. Many times individuals have their own agendas and ulterior motives that will not change their minds or alter their conduct.

The advent of social media has changed the entire communications environment. Social media has opened portals into everyone's personal interests, beliefs, private views, and even locations, thus creating a "fishbowl" environment where individuals are often judged by content without any contextual consideration. Further, individuals tend to" tweet or post" without much thought as to how such content will be perceived; there is no thought given to the probable or unintended consequences of that content. The very ability to and nature of a communication, if and when it becomes "viral," can have enormous consequences upon a person or their organization. Personal life and professional life have been merged into an inseparable state where everything, everywhere, every time is the functional equivalent of being official. Social media is vast, real-time, and permanent. One cannot take back what is posted, tweeted, or said and, he can't put the genie back in the bottle after the issue is formed and damage done.

Social media's evolution over the past several years has created an environment where leaders must be aware of and sensitive to their public behavior that could be captured by a smartphone camera and later posted to the Internet where it could be perceived by different people or groups in myriad manners depending upon specific beliefs or angles of view. These 21st century minefields and pitfalls can lead to massive credibility problems with one's ability to manage and lead. Consequently, one must be very sensitive to what, when, where, and how she posts, tweets, and uses. It is critical to use a structured method and careful manner when participating in social media. One can easily poison the well before she ever gets a bucket of water. Don't forge an adverse impression or perception on other; such a one can destroy one's ability to communicate and be respected.

However, and conversely and used correctly, the structured, planned, and narrowly tailored use of social media in today's communications sphere can be very beneficial providing it is thoughtfully measured in content, promotes accurate context, and stands properly implemented.

The Internet as a whole can be important as a means to innovate and further methods and means of communication. In 2009 I published an article titled, "The Major Incident Quadrahydral;" this article was an important part of my teaching at the time and provided an excellent summary for one of my classes. Shortly after publication of the work, a fellow supervisor and great friend called me to say that "Quadrahydral" was not a word and I should have consulted the dictionary before my proofreading. I was quick to tell him that I knew "Quadrahydral" was not a word, that I created it from "quad" – meaning four – and "hydral" – meaning sides. As a result of its failure to be in the dictionary, I could capitalize upon the utility of Google as a means for individuals to search and immediately find my material and thus supplement my classes without being required to be responsible for handouts. I had learned how to use new Internet search engines in relation to queries; I made it work best for me. This type of use is one that I deem both essential and worthwhile in reference to growing technology.

21st century technologies have effected every occupation, craft, and business; from the demise of record stores to the decrease in travel agents, digital technologies have changed the playing field. Today's thought process and tomorrow's focus will be based upon a "contextual security" guided by the particular habits and trends as observed by or traced through technological communication. Technology has closed doors in front of us and opened windows in other places; we have become much better in some areas and worse in others. The bottom line is we need to be alert, observant, and innovative, always trying to discover the best path through the modern complexities we travel. Embrace change and make change to adapt toward a more effective way; when it is meaningful find new waters. When it is not, hold your ship on course.

Key is opened minded assessment and analysis of safe, normal, and traditional philosophy; center risk on opportunity and awareness. More often than not, there is always a risk associated with the chance of reward. Lincoln said: "Better to remain silent and be thought a fool than to speak out and remove all doubt." Some circumstances require one to remain silent and simply listen. There are occasions where one needs to be silent and listen to exhibit the best message to his audience. Sometimes one needs to listen, learn, process, digest, and then research and think through the information before he forms or takes position. When one listens he exudes the automatic impression of care, of interest. This relates to an individual they, and what they say, are important.

Another issue in our modern culture is perception: different words mean different things to different people. Such demonstrates the importance of thinking "content and context" in one's communication. Words and how they are used in the workplace are important components to communication and the relationship between good communication and failure.

We always must think about our words before we use them; are they proper based upon the context of the situation? Once one uses a word, it's difficult to take it back or fix the communication if the word or phrase is insensitive, inflammatory, or hurtful to the receiver.

Again, this illustrates the importance of planning one's communications to her subordinates and the importance of knowing them and their situations within the workplace and community. One must be sensitive and empathetic when crafting her words to her subordinates, peers, and supervisors. Choose words well and remember how one says something can have more bearing than what she does. Sometimes, problems happen that are not necessarily due to the words or how they are used, but in their dual, or implied, meaning and labeling in an evolving vocabulary full of slang and flux.

On the lighter side, in the late 90's we were working an event at Tybee Island, Georgia. Our duties required us to drive from the beach to the roadways in the town. The Crown Victoria sedans we drove would not do on the beach. Our best bet was to rent ATVs from an equipment rental store nearby that had Kawasaki Mules available. But quickly, the issue became how to get the Mules from Garden City, Georgia to Tybee Island, a trek of over 20 miles through bumper-to-bumper Savannah traffic.

In the mid 90's, the Georgia forestry commission helped us haul ATVs with their "low-boy" trailers; luckily, there was a district office of the forestry commission in nearby Statesboro, Georgia that could help. I called the district manager and told him who I was and what we were being called to do in support of the Tybee Police Department. I told him we needed four Mules picked up in Garden City and transported by "low-boy" to the Tybee Police Department in several weeks.

The forestry supervisor grew very quiet and then replied, "Mr. Edwards, I don't think we can help you because of the liability issues of hauling mules through Savannah on a trailer without sides."

I said, "Well, we can tie them down."

He replied, "No, sir. That will not work; I wish we could help you, but we simply can't take that responsibility." I thanked him and hung up the phone, both puzzled and a little angered at his lack of cooperation regarding a simple request. Minutes later, he called me back and said: "Mr. Edwards, are you talking about real mules or four wheeled mules?"

We laughed, and I apologized for my lack of specificity and arrangements were made for our needs.

Sometimes it even isn't something we say that causes problems, but the inference based on presumed assumptions either by us or another party. Now that is a difficult thing to see looking from the outside in, but our only hope to mitigate this type of communication problem is make every attempt to sustain situational awareness by constant observation, constant listening, and constant consequence forecasting. The context of any event, issue, or situation is important; staying engaged with one's people is important. Take ego out of the loop. I've never had to tell someone I was the "boss," to threaten them to do their job with that almost ephemeral fear. I always ask before I tell and set the stage by explaining issues when I have the benefit of time.

I always welcome the "why" questions, and I am not affronted by them; "why" questions provide "teachable moments" and provide opportunities for mentorship and casting of vision. They also provide an appropriate time to influence, delegate ownership, and provide specific expectations. When one makes good communication a priority and works to see that it happens in a meaningful way, then performance is enhanced, people are motivated, and feelings of importance and influence are engendered.

Finally, do not get caught in the human frailty of holding grudges; falling into such traps can be and is severely detrimental to not only oneself, but of all those around him. The holding of grudges or designation of an "enemy" is a sure way to undermine one's abilities to be an effective communicator. He must incorporate the capacity to forgive and put his feelings to the side. He must strive to be objective and base his communication efforts upon his roles and responsibilities; no matter what the relationship, when it comes to organizational business and professional relationships, this is crucial.

Grudges must never dominate whether one communicates how one communicates. One can never limit her abilities and opportunities by limiting her sphere of influence because of conflict. Remember the value of humility – it ain't about you – and extend an olive branch; agree to disagree if necessary, but work to identify mutual areas of concern, promote and develop consensuses, and find common interests and common ground to dwell agree upon. R. Edward Freeman in his 1999 study said it best, "the finding of common ground limits conflict by creating agreement and the process taken by working together may heal old wounds and build positive relational pathways for future communication requirements."

As a rule, there are nine critically important steps to follow in the development of accurate and industrious communication skill sets:

1. Never gossip.

2. Never communicate indirectly or by proxy.

3. Never speak negatively about subordinates in front of other subordinates.

4. Never let relationships motivate or drive initial contact; treat everyone with respect and dignity and follow the proper roles, responsibilities, and jurisdictions.

5. Never put others in awkward, difficult communications positions.

6. Speak and be courteous with everyone encountered.

7. Respect the rank and the title of others in your communications. (both verbal and written)

8. Intentionally craft your communications for transparency. There is no such thing as "secret." People will talk and divulge what you say to them in confidence, be sure you always have sound motive, good facts and can stand by what you say and frame it in such a fashion to deal with when it becomes open to others. (Don't ever put out what you can't take coming back)

9. Give constant on-going, or at a minimum, weekly or bi-weekly status updates; keep subordinates and supervisors in the loop.

The method and manner we communicate matters, the words we choose and how we say them matter greatly. Use simple and understandable words; ensure you include the essential elements of information in your message to promote understanding and to get your theme across in terms others can grasp and relate too.

Always make message presentation more effective by increasing the chances of it being received and understood. If one takes great effort to craft his words well, use good non-verbal signals, explain the context, incorporate pathos, ethos, and logos, and use the right timing – kairos – then all he needs to do is foster the relationships with those around him.

Also, I have found over the years to use a simple and fundamental four step checklist to enhance our communication knowledge, skill and ability. I have termed this list the "structured communication cycle." I use the term cycle because the list never ends as long as we are engaged in communicating; just continues to go from step one through four and back to step one to cycle through again.

Here is the list:

- Aggressively listen
- Thoroughly analyze, evaluate, process and ensure understanding of the information
- Frame and formulate the proper feedback

- Relay on specifics, articulate your message in clear unambiguous language

I like to use one of our oldest occupations, farming, as an analogy. One's work place is her farm to produce the "fertile ground" requisite for planting the "important seeds" required for the right crop and best yield. This is just like communication. We till the fields of communication and deliberate toward sowing them correctly every time. Further, we must work to create and design structures, processes, and systems that help us to aerate the soil of communication so that the crop of understanding is cultivated correctly. We cannot lead, persuade, or influence if we cannot communicate.

Chapter Five:

"THE BURDEN OF MANAGEMENT"

You must develop the courage and maintain the fortitude to deal with people that do not do their jobs, make every attempt to mentor and develop them... but if they can't do the job, replace them. Those who do their jobs must be supported and rewarded. Your worst enemy in any work unit is mediocrity... <u>never ever settle for less than the best!</u>

"Leaders can either prepare or repair...
If you handle today correctly, tomorrow will take care of itself."
John Maxwell

The two quotes above are so true and accurate of leadership today, and if one follows the intent of these quotes, his management skills will be the better for it. Noah built the ark before the rain, and he lived because he followed his values. He followed his values because he chose to be right and do right. This concept is so simple, so basic, so elementary, so fundamental, and so very important. One cannot put a value on ethics and moral proactivity; such has been so throughout the ages and into the present. When leaders puts themselves in the position to remain ever mindful of the old adage, "the bell, the book, and the candle," or listen to warning bells, book laws, regulations, policies and ethics, and champion transparency and public exposure, they build their foundation on solid rocks instead of sinking sands.

The foundation of any leader is character built from integrity, fidelity, and credibility. One must have himself in line and in place before he can ever influence others. Further, he must do things the right way at the right time for the right reasons to reflect his character upon others. Then he must demonstrate, project, and embrace passion and desire to exemplify for others to understand and emulate. From this desire and passion comes the work ethic, the knowledge, the skills, and the abilities to be proactive and always prepared for what tomorrow may bring. Only then will he create a positive pathogen that transmit and infect all under his charge. They will not follow him because of his position, but because of who he is to them.

JFK once said, "A rising tide lifts all boats;" when one creates an atmosphere of pride and success among those under her charge and as a result an environment of perfection develops, everyone benefits. This phenomenon is the central component to creating a premier image, building inner and outer credibility, and establishing an exemplary reputation. Such will forge a positive perception that is the cornerstone to the success of any organization or mission in the 21st century arena.

The building of an in-house environmental culture driven by performance and motivated by individual ownership, sustained by team pride, tempered by respect and humility, and free from arrogance is the key to absolute success and consistent excellence. To reach this state of operational competence and exemplary production must be every manager's goal. It absolutely will not happen and cannot happen without dedicated, devoted, and proactive attention and action sustained by the burdensome and constant requirements previously outline for great leadership. It is and always will be about the "leadership." Managers must possess the governance skills, the unadulterated passion to be the best, and the persistent patience to get there.

This paradigm is created only by a leader's zero-tolerance for mediocrity, poor performance, poor behavior, and poor conduct, alongside the leader's vision, motivation, drive, influence, and persuasion to empower, delegate, give ownership, and promote purposeful results toward the ever-changing problem-laced responsibilities of navigating the 21st century work-scape of rapid communications, complex technologies, and storms of information.

The leader creates the "culture" of the work force and sustains such culture only by their constant and continuous work ethic, social skills, leadership influence, and results oriented management. Workers reflect their leadership and their leadership's performance behavior, and conduct.

At my first assignment as a supervisor, I took a 3x5 card and turned it lengthwise, and then I took a ruler and a red marker and drew a thin red line across the top fourth of the card. I then placed it in a vertical frame and atop my desk where everyone who walked in my office would see it. I made our motto at that office, "We stay above the red line," and then I preached vision, efficacy, and efficiency. I conveyed the importance of following good procedure and, of course, following the law.

Next, I demonstrated and modeled those standards to my people and had a zero-tolerance for anyone who strayed below that red line. This kept the Tri-circuit Drug Task Force out of trouble and built unit pride, model performance, and stellar reputation.

In those days, it was a huge amount of work to hire, train, and make ready an agent to be self-sufficient and productive. I made it a priority to get my eligible people promoted soon as I could; others would see what I was doing selling my folks for advancement to leave me to start all over again hiring, training and molding and they thought I was crazy to cut my own throat to lose my people. It proved to be the best motivator, for those present, those in my future, and those in my past spoke highly of that red line. I did not have the problems others had with personnel issues, investigative failures, or work ethics issues because of the quality of employee I was able to attract, manage, and sustain was exemplary.

You see, it is important to remember it's not the "bad apple" that ruins the lot; it's the barrel in which all the apples stay that ruins the lot. The "culture" of the work place, through the nature of leadership, determines organizational credibility, performance, and reputation.

Dr. Peter Drucker once said: "Management's function is to make a productive enterprise out of human and material resources." Only by and through prototypical leadership can the cornerstone be placed for building stellar management function. The key is to lead people to where they "self-manage." This is a simple proposition, but a tremendously difficult thing to create and sustain; however, it can be done when the leader preaches vision, provides clear expectations, creates an environment of ongoing two way open communication, and is constantly conveying anecdotes of purpose, thus forecasting possible consequences.

This is an absolute burden because of the constant changing forces afoot upon work, people, and leader. Just when one develops and molds an outstanding worker, something always changes. Situations between the task to be performed and the skills available to do it are always changing and evolving. Moreover, the environment of the work place rarely ever stays the same. People, resources, budgets, responsibilities, and requirements are fluid. Organizations must have the ability to adapt and change to become malleable molds of operations around such change. However, one thing never changes; the constant requirement and necessity for all organizations to contain exemplary leadership that creates outstanding management. The leader must have the skill sets and carry all the burdens we have discussed in previous chapters. As Everett T. Suters once said, "Management is an unnatural act"

It is tremendously difficult to manage oneself, not to mention to manage others. In supervision, we go from being responsible for just ourselves and personal actions, to being responsible to and for everyone and their actions. This is a giant leap of life changing effort clothed in uncertainty and covered with stressful positions at all times. We worry when we lose control; to trust and let go is not only difficult to do, but extremely scary. Risk is, and can be, a very intimidating and worrisome step, but everything involves risk; there can be no reward without the risk to achieve it.

Leaders must do three things up front to become great managers: First, get one's mind right. They must want and do accept responsibility and will take the risk to lead. Second, have the "fire in their belly," the desire to develop the passion for one's purpose and job. Third, do one's job to the absolute best of his ability.

Once the leader has developed these three components for a dedicated manager, she must then cross the bridge of no return, from worker to manager. She can never pitch her tent in the worker's camp again. There are two sides to the desk and she must always remain on the side of management. She can be empathic, kind, competent, a servant leader, and a great communicator, but if she does not separate herself from the "student body" and maintain her role and responsibility as "boss," she will "crash and burn."

One's employees need her to be aware, care about them and their work environment, and understand how work responsibilities affect them, how those around them who work with them affect them. A lot of "them's" and "we's," no "us's" One cannot be caught in the trap of being one of "them," but must endeavor to be himself. Critical to one is his objectivity, neutrality, fairness, and the perception of impartiality. To maintain this, the leader must be detached and free from any actions, events, or accounts that could cause a perception of subjective feelings regarding those under his charge.

Whether appointment to committees, special assignments, or promotions, the commander must make decisions and selections based upon a totality of circumstances style approach that is moral, legal, ethical, objective, and fair. A critical component to this is being organizationally and competence driven versus relationship driven.

Many people who are great workers and loyal employees may be excellent choices over others, but when seen through the lens of global objectivity may be relationship rich but competence poor. Moreover, these friends may place the commander in a position of like-minded subjective slants to view all issues.

Loyalty is a great virtue and positive relationships are the driver for great achievement but, sometimes a different view and opposite opinion are very healthy and beneficial. Also the credibility gained and reputation built by selecting the most qualified versus the most comfortable is a huge organizational motivator.

Like anything else in management there is no template, blue print or "cookie cutter" solution to this sometimes paradoxical and often mixture of positive and negative factors for the decisional equation. Furthermore, often these decisions are called upon to be "so situational" with a multitude of factors, issues and the anticipation of probable consequences.

A commander must remember they can always protect their command prerogatives and keep coalitions intact through demonstrating the personal qualities and professional strategy written about in this book.

The time will come often, when the commander will be called upon to make choices that will have huge impacts upon him, the organization and those who do the work, the better the choice the better chances for the result to be positive. Great measures of self-awareness, social- awareness, situational awareness must be combined with an objective, whole minded, and big picture thought process understanding that what's difficult to do today may be the best result for tomorrow. The key is an open minded evaluation of the candidates based upon facts and feedback over the relationship in combination with the situation, environments, expectations and expertise of the task required. In some jobs relational connections are huge, favor, trust, and loyalty are a premium, in most jobs work ethic and competency are far better. It is your job to know when to apply which expectations.

Leaders and managers must possess the character and sustain a reputation for fairness toward all employees at all times. Central to this ability is the application of three states of operation interwoven into the fabric of the supervision blanket.

1. Be open and forthright regarding the rules; create an atmosphere where everyone knows and understands the rules and your expectations as they apply to those rules.

2. Be consistent regarding how the rules are applied and enforced.

3. Be impartial when the rules are applied or enforced by demonstrating equality regarding all, no matter the relationship to the supervisor.

One must always regulate her thoughts, decisions, actions, and words under this rule of conduct. She can be a congenial person to all those under her supervision, but if she doesn't hold others accountable and make them do their jobs, her niceness will translate into "spinelessness," a negative managerial symptom spurred by indecisiveness, one who garners little to no respect, and one who negatively impacts all under her supervision every day. It is tremendously important to incorporate the burdens of self-awareness, competency, servant hood, and communication into one's leadership repertoire; however, she must insure she manages others under these behaviors in decisiveness and accountability.

There are times, too, when one must document poor performance and act on history to maintain the efficacy of his organization. It isn't about him or them; it's not personal; always keep it professional. It is about the organization, its performance, and its existence.

Relationships are important and critical to the leader's ability to influence and persuade, but relationships can change quickly under adverse circumstances; that's why relationships must remain in the proper professional context. "They are not your buddies, they are your people;" keep relationships credible and stay within proper work-sphere roles. Focus upon growing and developing professional, work related behavior and conduct and tailor decisions, actions, and coaching toward those ends. If one follows the laws of a servant leader, demonstrates competence, uses good communications skills, while as the same time staying self-aware with purpose, drive, and sensitivity, all will work out for the best possible ends.

In the first chapter, we placed an importance on the control of our emotions and the sensitivity and empathy we exude toward others. Remember? We can never deduct from the formula of human success the huge component of empathy and the central element of emotion. This leads me to two huge rules that one must never ever violate, but always follow in the instruction of actions with great precision. First and foremost, one must never "turn his head" from or nurture a "blind eye" for poor performance. Second, one must never ever attack another personally regarding poor performance; instead, describe the conduct and. Explain in detail why the action is sub-standard and what the consequences of such behavior are on the job or mission.

If one doesn't deal with issues when they occur, he loses a tremendous opportunity to change behavior and re-train an individual. Issues are better understood when fresh and in an environment robust with specific information, not restrained and diluted by the lapse of time and deterioration of facts and circumstances, lapses that lose meaning after mixed in other situational issues. If one does not deal with poor performance or bad issues forthright, such instances will only fester outside one's attention and evolve into bigger problems and larger issues that, by their very nature, may become too large and unstable to mitigate or eliminate in the long run.

It is no secret to many great leaders and managers that huge advantages exist when one possesses a specific and detailed structure in any organization. Structures create frameworks for individuals to mold into organizations. Remember in chapter two, when I gave the example of the grant funds for drug task forces that were awarded to good people with great intentions, but did not possess the policies, procedures, protocols, systems, and networks to provide an infrastructure to build upon and follow in their implementation and operations? As a result there were many failures that could have been avoided if such structures had been in place and have been trained upon.

The central element is the three phase use of policy in any management system incorporated into the organization. First, one must create sound, thoughtful, specific, thorough, and current policy, built from the ground up, encompassed in vision, and detailed in action. Second, all within the organization must be trained on the policy and possess an understanding and working knowledge of its rationale and how it should be implemented and followed. Third, managers must supervise the adherence of policy and enforce violations to maintain compliance and insure the policy of the organization and the customs of the organization are one in the same.

This three-phase structure will insure order, effectiveness, and efficiency while indemnifying oversight protection, insulation from adverse consequences, and transparency. This proactive structure, combined with a forward thinking mindset, prepares the organization for the future and provides the manager a blueprint for the present.

The leader must never become trapped in the mindset of, "The old way is the only way." The 21st century environment produces change at a rapid and contentious rate. Leaders and their organizations must not only keep up, but must also be devoted to outreach, research, and study to innovate and create new means, methods, and manners to accomplish task and enhance performance while mitigating liabilities. Never ever lower standards, "roll the dice," or risk reputation, integrity, or credibility as a leader or organization; if the issue afoot is moral, legal, and ethical, an open-minded analysis and evaluation of the facts and circumstances is a very productive and healthy option to choose. Always judge under the totality of all the facts and circumstances in an objective, open-minded fashion with the humility to aggressively listen to others but the discipline to apply the rules in accordance with exemplary critical thinking skills and decision making.

I have learned over the years that the best crystal ball is often a rearview mirror; however, things change and a huge part of that change is due to often unseen cultural, economic, and political forces that shift with the wind at different times for various reasons. I've learned I can't change those issues but must deal with them. How I am able to deal with them, and in the context I do deal with them, becomes very important.

The most significant skill I have found is education; if I can persuade and influence those under my command regarding understanding of the change, its potential effects upon the organization and them, and how together with their "buy-in" we can develop strategies and devise tactics to our advantage, I find the work to be much easier, much less daunting. This takes a tremendous amount of time to collect, analyze, interpret, and relay the facts in an action, reaction, and consequence context where all have a working understanding of the task and hurdles at hand.

One must prepare those under her command for the truth and benefits of adversity; difficulty produces growth and growth produces future competency. Colin Powell once said, "Optimism is a force multiplier." I fully believe the general is on point; I've seen the tremendous value of leadership when the "boss" models optimism by conduct, behavior, demeanor, statements, and action. It becomes addictive and a burden for those under their command to not be effected in a very positive and meaningful way.

Organizational awareness is huge, but without specific management specific to the problem area and/or person(s), the awareness translates into organizational stagnancy bound to the adverse influences of internal and external chaos. This illustrates the requirements that the Commander must always be engaged, connected, and involved in the people-component that drives the performance requirement of work. Management is the road map; leadership is the vehicle. To successfully set the course and complete the required journey one's mission demand, there must be both. Moreover, in today's environment, the journey's length, path, and duration are complicated by a specific and constant competitive oversight that demands results oriented objectives to consistently be met. One could be reactive and/or stagnant in the broad landscape of the 20th century, but in the narrow detailed terrain of the 21st century, only the proactive that adapt will survive.

But how does one remain proactive? Well, decision making, of course. We are required to make decisions every day. There is never a guarantee they are right; in fact, some are right while sometimes others are wrong. The first question should always be this: "Do we need to make a decision and should it be now?" The second, "Should we wait?" We know that time in the decision-making process can be our ally because as time moves forward, more facts develop and circumstances arise that can illuminate and impact the accuracy and efficacy of our decisions. However, we also know, and have learned, that sometimes the initiative is lost or an opportunity missed when we fail to make a timely decision. Sometimes, we may be able to recovery; however, most times the position of advantage is "gone with the wind."

The great Methodist theologian John Wesley had a saying: "Do no harm; do good and stay in love with God." This is instrumental for the commander to comprehend; if it is running well, if the chance for success is good, why do anything? Certainly add in the fact "that it ain't got to have your name or fingerprints on it, others are just as qualified or more to carry out the good Lords work.

We all possess the primal human desire for action; this is especially true when we inherit responsibility as Commander with the absolute knowledge and foresight that we will be judged by our actions or inactions by those who later evaluate us through the lens of hindsight as opposed to the real world dynamic of uncertainty and speculation rooted in limited facts. This motivation to act, what scholars call "the action imperative," is resolve fostered by the instinct to always move forward in an offensive posture instead of the patient stance required by time and observation. Patience is required to develop and mature an adverse situation into a more fortuitous situation through which one may base a credible forecast.

This is the great paradoxical dilemma the Commander finds himself in many times during the course of his leadership journey. I wish there were some template, protocol, or "cookie cutter" solution to this position of uncertainty, but sadly, none exists. Throughout antiquity and into the modern day, fate and history have often been determined by leaders who either choose to be proactive and take life by the horns, or those who choose to sit idly by, those who choose to let consequences come to them, to work themselves out. My experience has taught me to strive to gather all facts available, listen to those around me, and go with my instincts, to grab life by the horns.

Colonel Hal Moore, co-author of, "We Were Soldiers Once," and a celebrated army commander, once stated: "What am I doing that I should not be doing, and what am I not doing that I should be doing?" One must trust his instincts. Instincts and intuition give one an immediate estimation of a situation; trust your gut.

Often, issues in management are enigmatic; the same circumstances under a different context require different responses. In order to see and manage within the context of any given situation, one must be deliberate and determined to use all her resources and skills to see all the issues afoot, factor in all the facts, circumstances, situational and environmental features, then make interpretations and judgments upon there totality. Remember to demand "specificity" from all fact finders and insure their "basis of knowledge" or "how do they know" assumptions will destroy the validity of the process and result in poor results.

Moreover, one's efforts and processes will be watched, observed, digested, and modeled by those under her supervision. If the process is objective, thoughtful, pragmatic, and explained whenever a possible "teachable moment" is present, then those under one's command learn how one thinks and what one expects them to think. This pattern evolves into a consistency of ongoing beliefs, policy, and vision within the entire organization. The power of modeling consistency to regulate decisions and actions has a huge effect upon performance and results. Consistency in leadership demonstrates competency in the craft and organization and fosters outstanding outcomes in the work results of those to which leaders delegate jobs, tasks, and responsibilities.

When one promotes delegation, creates ownership, and provides consistent work philosophy, great results occur and become the normal course of business. This is why being consistent in vision, decision making, action is so critically important to build a great organization fueled by competent people that perform at their best levels.

Operations must be based on and rooted in consistent decision making complimented by legitimate policy and solid leadership support of those under one's charge. Never make a decision simply for the sake of making a decision; sometimes it is better to let the facts unfold over time. Then there are times that the failure to make a quick decision and initiate swift action can have terrible outcomes and adverse results. So how does the Commander move forward? What steps does one take? What process is the best to follow in the dynamic and fluid field of decision making that will burden any and all Commanders in their constant responsibilities and duties?

I am a firm believer that sound critical thinking skills begin with the leader's attitude. Foremost is the spirit of humility that must be present in all one does. I remember during my career in GBI I worked and supervised many major homicide investigations; I published a number of national and international publications regarding homicide investigative strategy and major case organization and investigation. I was always self-confident, eager, and prepared upon my arrival to a scene; however, my greatest ally was always the inner voice that spoke to me through my consciously disciplined and humble thought process. It consistently reminded me: "You learn every day and at every scene just how dumb you really are." This created an attitude that promoted listening, an open mind, and thirst for more information at all times.

Secondarily, after a humble state of mind comes an empathetic understanding of seeing things through others' eyes. Different people in different positions of responsibilities under different roles see things in different ways. I always tried to "walk in the other person's shoes" and attempt to listen and digest the information to promote my ability to understand how and why people saw things through the lens they did. We learned from rhetoric years ago the importance of the "pathos" – Greek for suffering or experience rhetorically refers to the focus on values and/or beliefs associated with emotional appeal or sympathies – that drives an audience to interest and attention or is the foundation that fixes their strong positions.

After fully realizing these two positions of insight and reflection, one can finally move into the traditional and pragmatic rules of critical thinking. I have boiled these rules down to the following five steps, five steps that have benefited me for many years:

1. *A constantly objective and open mind free from emotion and belief based bias:*

   Often our beliefs trump our ability to evaluate facts and evidence in an objective and meaningful way. It is easy to be a victim of what Dr. Kim Rossmo of Texas State University refers to as, "Belief perseverance," an affliction where one's beliefs close his mind to existing or new evidence that refutes his longstanding beliefs. Fact finding should be a deliberately skeptical process that proceeds from general to specific in scope when evaluating and analyzing the totality of all data and circumstances.

2. *An aggressive and proactive quest for research, inquiry, and study to identify all available facts and circumstances within a sound foundation of the veracity of all information is key:*

   One must be very dedicated and devoted toward learning all he can, as soon as he can, to insure what he learns is credible and reliable. Always remember: 99 percent of all preliminary information is either misinterpreted, embellished, exaggerated, or totally false 99 percent of the time. This is why we must always ensure our collected information contains a credible or reliable "basis of knowledge." Always ask, "How do you know?" Make this question an essential part of you repertoire during all inquiry!

3. *All conclusions must be based upon facts; all claims must be supported by facts:*
   Evaluate, analyze, examine, and weigh the specifics, then make sure any and all conclusions stand on those specifics processed.

4. *Work with an objective process of reasoning; include others' opinions in the process:*
   There is wisdom, not weakness, in sharing decision-making issues when you have the benefit of time. Others opinions, ideas, and theories are imperative to promote better critical thinking as they foster open-mindedness, alternate possibilities, and alternate conclusion identification. Moreover, multiple minds always see more and cover more than one. Welcome debate and "devil's advocate" style feedback and commentary.

5. *Reflect on conclusions for alternate theories, ideas, and questions; anticipate both intended and unintended consequences:*
   If one has the time, always invest in provocative thought reflection to uncover additional issues, identify potential problems, form additional questions, and forecast possible consequences of action, reactions, or, when applicable, inaction. Further, reflection over one's conclusion promotes certainty and identifies uncertainties; such uniquely prepares one for the often quickly changing environments or situations that follow decisions.

Additionally, Sir Winston Churchill had a great system as well, something he called the "Five Distinct Truths Governing Decisions;" these correlate with the above five steps and, in conjunction, create an almost foolproof schematic for the critical thinking paradigm.

1. There is a full authority.

2. There is a reasonable prospect of success.

3. Greater interests are not compromised.

4. All possible care and forethought is exercised in preparation.

5. All vigor and determination is shown in execution.

Churchill said: "To condemn operations simply because they involve risk and uncertainties...some operations can and ought to be made certainties; others belong to the class where one can only balance the chances and action must proceed on a preponderance of favorable chances."

Decisions must be fact driven and evidence based. Times will come where one will have to make assumptions. Some will be based upon the whole picture and some based upon half. Often, assumptions are a necessary path toward discovering truth and making preliminary decisions that lead to larger, more informed decisions. There are always different views and perspectives, different interpretations and conclusions. It is important how one goes about making decisions because these assumptions can be well intended with the best result sought, but ultimately wrong; decisions can always produce unintended or adverse consequences. It is natural and human to make mistakes from assumptions.

As I have stated now many times, the purpose of this book is to provide the commander with a resource pool and tool chest to reach into for everyday use in maneuvering through the quagmires in management. I am convinced this emotional intelligence based, competent, communicative and servant leader is by far the best course. However, there are times where "situational leadership" when applied the right way, at the right time, and in the right place has been of benefit to me.

A prerequisite and important skill set for all managers in order to lead effectively is a working knowledge, in-depth understanding and the ability to functionally apply The Situational Leadership Model that was developed by Paul Hershey and Ken Blanchard years ago. This model will be of great benefit and of continuous utility in one's endeavors to match the proper management and leadership style to the proper set of facts and circumstances that arise from the employee and the task to be accomplished. Without "getting into the weeds" the models components are as follows:

The leader adapts to different work place situations at different times with different job requirements by adjusting their specific task accomplishing relations and behaviors specific to the set of circumstances involving the employee, based upon the employees motivation, readiness and competency to do the specific task or tasks the job requires. In other words we know the importance that I have driven home time and time again in this book of training and developing your subordinates, then delegating to them the task at hand, and letting them possess the ownership in that task given to perform. This is the formula for success, but sometimes the task changes, or the environment or landscape around it changes and we must ensure our subordinates retain the knowledge, skill and ability with the right motivation and readiness or preparedness level to do the job well.

Hersey and Blanchard's model starts with the employee's preparedness level in four categories as it relates to their development stage and motivation level:

- Low competence and low commitment
- Low competence and high commitment
- High competence and low commitment
- High competence and high commitment

Then, the leader matches and adapts their leadership behaviors to the above specific categories by applying the below styles to above situations:

- Telling employees
- Selling employees
- Participating with employees
- Delegation to employees

In the burden of competence I wrote about the importance of learning your job. The internet is full of credible work regarding this important topic, make it a priority to study and learn this model so it becomes a tool in your leadership repertoire.

Once I was required to step in as an acting SAC in an alternative office. During a debriefing prior to the current SAC leaving, he told me of one particular agent that he had denied a secondary employment request because of low activity and how such would be an issue that would require my attention. He regretted it being so, but it would a necessary issue.

This employee was a veteran agent who had been in drug enforcement for years, enjoyed a good reputation within our agency and among the local law enforcement, and was entrenched in a particular workplace mindset. He was smart and well mannered; I had always admired him and enjoyed his company when provided.

After I stepped in as official "acting" Commander, I noticed that the case records showed, as the previous SAC had mentioned, the agent's activity was very low. I made it a point to travel to our sub-office to talk with him and hear his reasons for the low activity. He told me that he worked a very corrupt county, and that the police officials were never cooperative or participatory with GBI operations. He said he could never obtain information or develop informants because of this county's culture of "hands off and blind eye" law enforcement. His story was reasonable and worth efforts to find a "level playing field" for him to demonstrate that his low activity was not a result of an energy crisis but caused by a sterilized and detached environment forth with internal barriers and pitfalls.

I found an opportunity and devised a plan to give this agent a territory that was not only target rich with violators, but also blessed with excellent local police full of energy and vigor. The new assignment was made.

The carrier's bow may have turned into the wind, but no planes ever launched; the agent's activity remained low and worse, I now had "local sources" complaining that they provided credible and actionable information, but he would do nothing. When I approached the agent, he always met me with an excuse for the inaction; but the devil is always in the details and the specificity of my information did not match the responses from his.

My first thought was: "He's lazy; there's something going on in his personal life, or he's mad over the previous denial of his secondary work request." In the original meeting for his new assignment, I told him that I wanted to get his activity up so I could approve his previous request, so I could help him with the employment issue; I knew times were hard and every little bit helped. Nonetheless, we had to do mission before any of that could happen.

I asked myself, "Why can't he do the job?" After much searching, it came to me: this was a veteran agent working in an office surrounded many much younger and less experienced agents. He had dignity and pride; he wanted to live up to his reputation within the agency. I knew he had come to Savannah with vast undercover experience and general investigative experience, but when was the last time he had been required to write a search warrant? The construction and application of a search warrant is a very technical and procedural thing, and one has to know how to do it; unlike riding a bicycle, if one doesn't do it, he loses it.

So I had a meeting with him, asked him when he had last constructed, and executed a search warrant. Not to my surprise, I found that he had not done so in years; he had lost his confidence and skill sets to do so. I knew his position, stature, and pride within the organization would prevent him from ever acknowledging this or asking for help. He is human and did not want the perceived embarrassment, especially among the junior agents around him, to usurp his clout. Moreover, I knew I needed to preserve his self-esteem while at the same time giving him the tools he needed to produce the necessary skill sets to do the job. After a day of refresher training, his search warrant competency returned. As a result, his activity went up and cases were made because he now had the requisite tools and knowledge to accomplish the mission and produce results.

The lesson is this: it's easy to assume the first impression or the simplest answer; however, like in this case, further inquiry, methodical process management, and problem solving mindsets can be a light unto one's path, one that yields constructive results. In this case, the agent was smart and proud, but handicapped at a certain time by a certain skill that, on the outside, conveyed laziness although it ultimately was not. Nonetheless, it would have been easy to assume so and guess what the impact of that assumption would be and where it could lead? I would bet on absolute tragedy for a good employee and the organization. As such, this employee corrected his skills and changed his behavior; after all of this, he received his secondary work approval and benefits within the agency. We both accomplished our goals.

It is work to manage, and management for human beings is very unnatural; it does not just come to you. In fact, you're born with those frailties of the human condition, ones that constantly work against you as a manager, especially in the servant-leader context as human nature is, at its core, selfish. Different managers have different angles of view based upon their nature, their training, their education, and their experiences. As a result, it becomes incredibly important for all of the burdens we have covered to come to play in the overall management perspective and process.

I remember when I was the Commander of the Drug TaskForce and my supervisor called me regarding an order of strobe lights I had previously made to put in our agents head and tail lights. My boss questioned my decision to purchase plain-clothes narcotics officers such lights for their vehicles.

I told him my reason was that the agents in question had requested them following a near hit-and-run while conducting a drug arrest; I continued by stating that I believed such lights would create a safer scenario for the public and our agents. My "boss" then advised that he had concerns with approving the light packages because such packages may give the agents more incentive and motivation to work misdemeanor traffic violations and conduct traffic stops in unmarked cars, thus causing complaints and problems. This perspective was based upon the angle of view predicated by his past managerial experiences.

I told him that if he approved the lights for my people and problems surfaced as a result of them improperly conducting traffic stops, then the problem was neither the lights nor the agents; the problem was me and my poor ability to manage. The agents needed the lights; working traffic in an unmarked car was a violation of policy. My job as a manager was to insure the agents had the resources they needed to perform their jobs in compliance with our policies and procedures.

Finally, my "boss" approved the lights; we had them installed, and I had a staff meeting that covered, in detail, the organization's policy. Moreover, for transparency, I articulated my "boss'" concerns, my vision, and my expectation regarding compliance. We never had a problem.

Good leaders must transform their efforts into good management and good management calls for specific knowledge, ongoing involvement, and continuing oversight. The easy way out must never be taken. Supervision is not easy; it demands one to stay aware and to stay on top of issues and events. When a manager paints with a broad brush to limit his risk and reduce his labor, he cheats those under his command; the performance possibilities that favor the organization nose-dive. Devoted managers look for ways to bend the boundaries to provide greater freedom, to access initiatives within their staff's environment.

As I wrote in the chapter Burden of Servant-hood about the importance of an objective, fair, and well documented job performance evaluation and how such an evaluation process must be blended into the mentorship and coaching process, I used the evaluation process to help me motivate and "show off" my great employees. Create opportunity for one's most competent, the one most deserving of promotion and reward. During the formal evaluation process I took the most time to document great and good things. My performance evaluations were always thick, crammed with specific documentation of the exemplary work and behaviors of my subordinates. I used the evaluation meeting as a time to show my employee how much work I put into documenting what they did right, and to provide other supervisors the opportunity to understand chosen employees' worth and importance to the organization and its purpose.

I carried 3x5 cards in my front shirt pocket every day, and when I saw great work, difficult work, great conduct or behavior, I would write that employee's name on the card, describe the performance and behavior in detail, and file it away for my subsequently scheduled written evaluations. Then, at time of the evaluation, I would transfer the dates and information from the card to the evaluation document. Thus, I had a means – the agency formal evaluation document – and I had a method – the required formal evaluation meeting between supervisor and subordinate that officially provided documented praise from me to them and up the chain of command in order to confer on them positive exposure, specific credit, and deserved recognition to their whole command and leadership structure; this was a tremendously positive means of encouragement and motivation and an important and meaningful part of leadership.

Whether required by one's agency annually, bi-annually, or quarterly, job performance evaluations should be an on-going and daily occurrence where the manager looks to train, encourage, model, and coach and correct when possible. Following the evaluation process, comes a responsibility to dedicate time if applicable to adequate re-training, re-tooling, and re-development.

Performance evaluations are one of the most important tools in the leadership and management process. One uses the utility of the evaluation to motivate, sustain, and change behavior and use its documentation to discipline and terminate. Everyone expects a leader to be an empathetic, caring, and servant-centered individual, but also hold the expectation that a leader does her job and terminates those who do not work or fail to have the skills and abilities to do the job.

There are seven important rules for the evaluation process:

1. Ensure agency approved structures and processes are document-ed; employee job performance evaluations must be supported by sound personnel policy reviewed and approved regularly by the agency attorney.

2. Corrective interviews, error documentation, and problem-examining documentation must correlate with poor performance, improper conduct, or abnormal behavior.

3. Continuous mentoring and coaching is a priority; provide constant positive feedback both to encourage and correct.

4. Mentors should always be candid, honest, and forthright; feedback with genuine devotion toward professional development and growth within the craft and the organization is required.

5. Never surprise subordinates with conduct, behavior, or work results; transparency is key. Your employees must always know where they stand. How can you expect them to change if you are not open and honest with them regarding their performance?

6. Ensure performance evaluation remains ongoing and engaged; see step five.

7. Document good performances similarly as poor performances; ensure subordinates have read, understand, and signed-off on any documentation regarding performance.

When dealing with subordinates in the corrective paradigm, leaders always talk in private and follow these aforementioned steps. First, find something to say good about something they have done or tried to do well for the organization. It is important to capture their attention through positive means and the human condition of self-worth...remember to never attack the person personally – it is never personal, always keep it professional. Second, stick with describing the poor conduct or improper behavior. Third, described the poor performance in specific detail and how that conduct adversely effects the job performance expected, explain and outline the consequences from such conduct and how it adversely relates to them, the mission and the agency. Fourth, give examples of proper, desired and acceptable behavior of conduct in the scenario or issues then tie in your expectations and solicit their input regarding those expectations you have outlined to them. Fifth, develop solutions to their problems and provide understanding of their roles and responsibilities as they relate to their job description. Design and develop a performance plan incorporating what you can do as a supervisor to help them, whether additional training, specific task mentorship or resources. Sixth, obtain their "buy in" and commitment to your expectations their responsibilities to the organization. Seventh, agree upon the importance and need of a future meeting time to get together to follow up upon their performance and job results to ensure their success as a valued member of the organization.

Now, this process can and does happen many times with great employees for no pragmatic reason, specific utility, or demonstrative reason to document anything whatsoever; this process becomes part of the ever evolving and ongoing process of supervision that is a central component of leadership and management. It just is. Moreover, great Commanders reach a point where all of their subordinates expect this process as a part of their work journey.

However, when one begins to notice this corrective process is no longer effective and the subordinate loses the ability to grow and develop, or the will and commitment to adapt, to change his conduct and behavioral patterns, then one must put the pen to paper and document the process well.

A leader's job is to ensure the expected job performance is completed; she exceeds and her organization exceeds when she ensures subordinates prosper by doing exceeding expectations and providing premier results. Great results can't happen if Commanders and executives retain sub-standard employees. If a subordinate can't do the job, they must go elsewhere, and it is your duty and obligation to document the facts and circumstances in a results oriented, fair, and accurately objective context driven by partnership between supervisor and subordinate.

There will be troubling times and difficult people in the evaluation process no matter what, where, or when. This is a given. My experience has been that these times are few between, but they do happen. When one encounters an angry, aggressive, or problematic employee, he must endeavor to start off as positively, patiently, and calmly as possible. Remember to refrain from doing anything they could be interpreted as a personal attack; deal only with the correction of their behavior or conduct. If there is any way to highlight something they have done positive, illuminate that before the conversation begins.

And after all of this, integrate the following steps into your evaluation meeting:

1. Aggressively listen to your subordinate; promote devoted attention to them and what they say. Be sure to actively demonstrate non-verbal's.

2. Tell them you want to take specific notes because what they say is important to you

3. Repeat what they say back to them; when they hear from you what they said and know you heard them and understand what was important to them, they tend to open themselves to a wider array of possibilities.

4. Evaluate issues, problems, or opinions before providing tailored feedback.

If subordinates don't have the desire to work and passion for their job, they will not perform the work, promote the purpose, or provide the results necessary to accomplish the task required by the organization. One's job as Commander is to create and sustain the office, work place, and work unit "culture" with her staff to ensure that objective, fair, and ongoing feedback is current with job performance evaluations through mentorship, coaching, and engagement. Evaluating policy and company processes are very important and critical to complete as required, but the rationale behind them is an everyday assessment of performance, not a designated time to "just do a job."

The prime danger, central component, and chief cause of complacency shares its nexus with incompetence, inefficiency, ineffectiveness, and failure to challenge the status quo. One who dwells upon and takes satisfaction in the preservation of the existing state of affairs and, as a result, remains resistant to change will ultimately become the perfect-storm-catalyst to poor performance and sub-standard behaviors, conduct that will ultimately lead to absolute failure.

Leaders such as this will also miss opportunities and chances for the capturing of great initiatives, programs, projects, or work; they lose the advantage of mitigating risk and failure. Change, whether good or bad, is oftentimes equally resisted because of the required work needed to adapt and evolve, or research and educate within the development of additional knowledge and skills. No person or group ever reached a point in life where they knew it all, could do it all, or saw it all.

Those who never settle for mediocrity in their leadership character are able to proactively see, identify, adapt, and seize the initiative that will promote good results and remain on "the cutting edge;" they will also gain the respect and develop the reputation for garnering and sustaining excellence. Those who possess a passion for their job as a result of their confidence in the purposeful work they do and, by design, make a tremendous effort to research their craft, educate themselves, and enhance their professional growth, will never be satisfied with the "status quo," but strive always to evolve, adapt, and change to become as effective and efficient as possible.

Never become a stagnate leader trapped in the quagmire of job mediocrity; understand, accept, and perform at only the highest levels; if one does, he will become the principle cause of a work place destined to failure, the principle doom of a "culture "of complacency and incompetence that will ultimately end in embarrassment and leadership change.

There are times bad things happen to good people; there are times good people make bad decisions and behave faultily; there are times where there are pure accidents. However, at the end of the day, the Commander is responsible. Remember, one can never control people and the intersection of where they decide and act, what incidents and events will or will not occur. A great leader can take proactive measures to mitigate risk though the many leadership strategies we have already outlined. History and experience has taught me that more often than not it's not the issue or incident that impacts you as much as how you handle it. Things will happen; the question is this: "How will you see it and manage it?"

In October 2011, Vernon Keenan, the Director of the GBI, and Dawn Diedrich, Director of GBI's legal services, did a presentation in Chicago at the International Association of Chiefs of Police Conference titled, "Managing Agency Errors." They developed their course content from in-the-field experience, experience that dealt with controversial events and major errors in judgments, work operations, or behaviors by those under the Director's command. Vernon focused upon the ethical, practical, historical, and consequential side, while Dawn evaluated the legal side. They provided some great advice and set tremendously high standards for management to follow and for Commanders to enforce.

Here is what they outlined:

1. **Credible Investigation:** Ensure specific and thorough fact-finding; conduct independent investigations in a professional manner using professional methods; leave no stone unturned.

2. **Accurate Findings:** Ensure the results of any investigation are both accurate and complete; all findings are based upon objective conclusions supported by specific facts.

3. **Documentation:** Ensure all facts, circumstances, statements, and issues are properly documented in an appropriate manner; review all such documents for accuracy and relevancy.

4. **Executive Summary:** Review all findings involving your legal representatives, subject matter experts, command staff members, and involved parties before signing off on any executive summary.

5. **Full Disclosures:** Focus upon transparency for all.

They pointed out that we could never eliminate mistakes, errors, or adverse incidents or events because we are human, fallible. We could and can, however, avoid becoming part of the problem; this comes from how we handle mistakes, errors, or bad decisions. We need to be firmly resolved to never lie, mislead, or obfuscate. We cannot control or change what has happened, but we can control and influence how we address and manage the problem.

They went further to point out that history shows that executives or commanders who follow the below listed behaviors not only fail, but lose their leadership positions, tarnish their credibility, and often ruin their reputation.

1. Ignore the report of a problem.

2. Disallow the appropriate agency command staff input.

3. Conduct perfunctory investigations.

4. Fail to act or discipline when appropriate.

5. Demonstrate a lack of transparency.

Vernon and Dawn's course ought to be mandatory training for every executive, Commander, manager, supervisor, and leader. Those who translate their philosophy into action will be the better for it. My belief in Vernon and Dawn's training content comes from what I believe to be the same passion Vernon and Dawn have, which is a sincere loyalty and supreme devotion to values.

Several months ago, I was talking with Roy Harris, a dear friend and a great leader, who is a Chief Deputy Sheriff. Roy and I go way back; he was one of the smartest and most thorough supervisors I ever had. He has retained his same love and passion for the craft for over 40 years. During our conversation, we acknowledged what a huge advantage we had when we retired from management positions in the GBI and accepted Chief Deputy Positions in other agencies, and how carrying those professional values with us positioned us to provide our Sheriff's deputies, jailers, and staff with the type management they expected and deserved. Moreover, we came equipped with a compass that always pointed us to the true north; even when we were tempted to stray off other directions, we never did; our GBI experience kept us on course.

We knew we were not better than anyone else; we just were able to focus and frame issues in a responsible and measured way by factoring our values and experiences into the overall equation. Equally important, we both knew the value and importance of the outstanding deputies we managed or Sheriff's we served and how we learned from them regarding their angles of view, work, dedication, and special skills sets they had and used so well and how they too, had values that served as a "blue print' for their job performance. Bottom line, wherever you come from or go to, your values are important.

Dr. Joycelyn Pollack, in her captivating textbook, "Ethical Dilemmas and Decisions in Criminal Justice," tells the story of Captain Scott Waddle, Commander of the submarine U.S.S. Greenville, who was part of a tragic accident in February of 2001. After the accident, Waddle spoke to his crew on the ship's intercom and said: "Remember what you saw; remember what happened; do not embellish; tell the truth and maintain your dignity." Against his lawyer's advice, Waddle gave up his right to remain silent at his military tribunal where he said, "It's the right thing to do…I'm solely responsible for this tragic accident, and for the rest of my life I will have to live with the horrible consequences." Eventually, he received a letter of reprimand and ended his naval career. Waddle said that the values of honesty and responsibility he had learned as an Eagle Scout drove his decisions and conduct.

One can never turn back the hands of time or turn a blind eye to the facts; however, one can deal with what has happen in the best way possible and take the high ground, do what is right. It's tough to take the heat and tougher to suffer the consequences, but as Scarlet said in *Gone with the Wind*, "Tomorrow is another day."

Not too long ago, I was traveling through a small town when my wife and I decided we would choose a fast food chain to grab a quick burger; we pulled into the drive through, made our order of two burgers and two soft drinks, and twenty minutes later we made it to the pick-up window where I asked the young server if a 20 minute wait was normal?

Her manager, who interrupted her, was quick to tell me that: "Next time I needed to call ahead and order before coming through the drive in window."

I replied: "Isn't the reason of a drive through to make a "to go" order?

He replied, "We have been busy and gotten behind"

I told him I was glad he did not work at NASA, paid for my cold burgers, and left, resolved I would never stop at that particular store anymore. It was clear this manager's focus was on himself and his store, not on my needs or me; His needs weren't even on his employee.

In any business, those who remain customer focused and dedicated toward providing the absolute best products or services succeed where others fail. A great Commander is always dedicated and devoted toward performing at the very best for those served.

I remember when I was teenager working as a bag boy at our local grocery store on the weekends. I would become furious when late shoppers would come in the store at night, minutes before our scheduled closing time. These "interlopers" who, I believed intentionally waited until the last minute to buy goods that they had all day to buy, would cause us all to frown and other ghastly displays of body language. As they would leave, we would sigh in relief and groan in anger toward their taillights. Needless to say, these people never got good service, care, or attention; instead, they were lucky not to get their bread squashed.

This story illustrates how selfish, small minded, and wrong we were. The closing time on our door was a perimeter for business, not an absolute with special terms or conditions tailored toward our convenience and after work plans. Our job was to provide the same service to everyone, every time, and anytime they came through that door. The fact they were late and made us late didn't matter; what mattered was a smile, kind face, and courteous and meaningful service. We worked for that store to service them to, ensure customers would come back to that store time and time again, regardless of the hour. We didn't have our priorities right or our responsibilities inline. Moreover, we were self-oriented, not service-oriented. I learned my lesson and changed my perspective, finally realizing my job came before my wants, and the heart of most jobs surrounds service, how one perceives it, embraces it, and performs it.

Management takes courage, fortitude, and understanding; you are responsible to do the difficult things because it is your job. You can't command if you can't manage, and if you can't manage, you can't lead.

Remember, always to be "servant and service" oriented and devoted to your clients, stakeholders and the organizations mission. This is the true north that will give you the direction, build your values, and shape your vision as a Commander. It is always easier to see and live in your world than the worlds of others; you must constantly and consistently sustain the environmental and situational awareness to see the difference between the two.

Finally, the advantage of sustaining a proactive mindset as a manager is when you manage what could happen before it does happen; then you have an opportunity to influence and bend the future in your favor toward your anticipated result. One of the hardest working agents and best supervisors I ever knew was Bob Ingram. Inspector Ingram was the Director's "go to" person when work units got in trouble and managers failed. Bob's internal investigations were always thorough and accurate in the results and conclusions. I remember talking with Bob regarding what he had seen and learned as a reoccurring theme in these inquiries. Bob's response to me was short, basic, resolute and deliberate. He said "John the leader did not do his job." It is that simple; you must do your job in leadership position, management role and command responsibility.

You will be held accountable down the road. Manage in a fashion to manage yourself first. Never be late, always be early, never make your crisis some else's emergency, and strive to sustain calmness instead of fueling chaos. You can never ever become indifferent or careless, but must be caring, sincere, and aware always placing a high priority on work ethic and high performance. Never refrain from wanting the truth and striving to obtain it. Deal with issues, don't think they will go away; they will just fester and become worse. Take care of your administrative and operational responsibilities in a thorough, accurate, complete, and timely manner. You can be the best leader, but if you fail as a manager you fail at your job.

Commanders must have the benefit of exemplary documentation and records that exceed the organizations standards. The secret to this is simple: love your job, know your job, and do your job. If you follow these three rules you will have the desire, competence, courage and fortitude to your job well. There will be hard work, sacrifice, and difficult times, but there will also be rewards.

Along our Georgia coast there are beautiful live oak trees, these evergreens are old and majestic but as you observe them, you notice they bend in the direction of coastal winds never breaking. It was said that General Washington was fond of this tree for ship construction in our early Navy because of the wood's strength. In fact, the famous USS Constitution, or "Old Ironsides," was constructed with Southern live oak lumber. The beautiful and useful live oaks grow strong under the tension of the constant coastal winds much like how the most sought after stone, the diamond, is a result of simple coal remaining under vast pressures deep in the earth for long periods. Diamonds are used to represent our most cherished time and used to dig in places where no other material can stand up to the stress. These materials become what they are by facing adversity. Like these two materials, each commander grows and develops into their best form only as a result of running toward difficult and labor intensive duty.

EPILOGUE

**"A compass, I learned when I was surveying... it'll point you true
north from where you're standing, but it's got no advice about the
swamps and desserts and chasms that you'll encounter along the
way. If in pursuit of your destination you plunge ahead, heedless of
obstacles, and achieve nothing more than to sink in a swamp... what's
the use of knowing true north?"**
-Tony Kushner: Lincoln.

This quote from Spielberg's epic is so appropriate to the demonstration
of the complex nature of progression through adverse conditions in the
work place. Today's Commander must be equipped with the wisdom,
skills, and talents to maneuver through the issues, incidents, and events
of the day, month, or year to meet the goals and objectives of any organization. One can't promote a "My way or the highway attitude" or tear
through the status quo, blindly moving forward while following some
arbitrary roadmap set in place by any not connected to the everyday

players. A Commander must use his head and his heart to measure, feel, and move his way through multiple obstacles on the way to achieving the goal sought; it is almost never done alone.

Influence and persuasion is an integral part of one's ability to command and obtain the results required. Many times, "It ain't what you want, it's what you've got," and then it becomes how one uses it that matters. My hope and prayer is that this book will serve as a reference to help through this continuing journey of command and responsibility, and the information herein will be of meaningful and continuing utility to anyone and everyone seeking to become a better commander.

It is clear from academic research that evolution of the work place is real and, in combination with the proliferation of real time information propelled by modern technologies, Commanders, managers, and leaders must be self-aware, self-disciplined, self-managed, and socially skilled. Science and craft support this all important notion. The key lies in dedication and devotion, in the priority one places in achieving and sustaining the requirements that make that responsibility reality. So much relies upon who we are, what we do, and how we go about doing it. The mindsets and the values we hold dear will set the course and the pace of our journey through the position of authority and responsibility; these factors, more often than not, determine how long we hold that position and what we made of it while there.

Chapter One outlines what is arguably the most challenging burden: to be able to see oneself and judge himself accurately while, at the same time, managing himself correctly; these are difficult issues, but required before one can effectively command and lead. To manage others, one must first be able to manage himself.

Time, is the essential ingredient in the recipe for the chances of success in any given scenario. Anywhere, on any occasion you devote your time to a project, person, problem or issue, you invest in the probability of it being better. Whether it is a particular aspect of your work, your relationships with friends, or your responsibilities with family, time is a critical component to development, growth, positive change and the ability to react to the tensions caused by having to adapt to an ever changing and evolving world.

Competence, the subject of Chapter Two, is also a tremendously difficult sphere to continuously inhabit, but its requirements are more labor intensive than psychologically difficult. Competency requires redundancy and desire. The great author Shelby Foote once said: "I can't begin to tell you the times I discovered something while I was looking for something else." The quest for researching to learn creates an environment that intends to capture so many other things that foster additional learning and thus, and by proxy, illuminates additional information on the original situation, at least most of the time. Understanding this is critical in the 21st century rat race. Decisions we make today often become better investments in positive results if our decisions are tailored toward a probable future opportunity, risk, consequence, or result.

Bill Gates put this in perspective when he said: "We always overestimate the change that will occur in the next two years and underestimate the change that will occur in the next ten…Don't let yourself be lulled into inaction." The message here is to drill deep into the information, see 360 degrees, stay current, aware, and abreast of what's happening around you.

Servant-hood, like self-awareness, requires that same objective, that same "deny-self" mentality, to insure we live what we talk and do what we say. Moreover, servant-hood is a disciplined framework that requires a constant consciousness to remain within that sphere of attitude where outreach to and for others takes priority at all times, good or bad.

To be understood and accepted is a true blessing and tremendous benefit toward any human interaction; communication is the glue that holds human organization and coordination together, and further good communication insures better implementation of task and plans and increases the probabilities of the sought after result. As we outlined in Chapter Four, communication requires planning and work. The great communicator enhances performance, mitigates problems, and develops relationships that grow and prosper. It is an absolute burden to communicate because the pressure to do it at the right time, in the right place, and to the right people for the right reasons remains constantly in flux.

Lastly, Chapter Five puts the rubber on the road; the burden of management is tough because of its unnatural tendencies contradict the grain. Tolerance to understand and self-control to be quiet and watch, depending upon the people involved, their willingness to perform, their ability and skill to accomplish the task and the situational context afoot, is paramount.

Good leaders fulfill their obligation to manage and good managers positively motivate and influence those they lead. A great Commander does both well; she maintains sound performance and achieves solid results. The constant changes, responsibilities, and requirements make management an absolute burden weighing upon the commander every day.

In the June 2013 edition of "Ideas in American Policing," which featured the article, "Improving Police: What's Craft Got to do With It?" Author James J. Willis states: "The evidence-based movement has captured the attention of government and generated excitement about the possibilities for reform, so this is a good time to use science to cultivate and test what accumulated experience has to offer."

Oscar Wilde once remarked that the proper basis for marriage was mutual misunderstanding that happiness could not be found within its bounds. This does not have to be the case for craft and science with one looking past the other and lamenting missed opportunities. A fuller appreciation of the qualities each brings to the other promises a much more satisfying and enduring relationship."

Academic research is very important to the way we identify and determine best practice. Over the years, many different professions have embraced "evidence based" practices and as a result have become much more effective at what they are charged to do. Craft, or the body of experience, has also played a significant role, both good and bad, regarding how organizations and professions determine best practices.

Leadership paints with a broad brush across the canvass of every profession and organization; methods and manners used to promote excellent leadership become investments that will surely pay large dividends to any organization and profession. Thus, I would be remiss if I did not explore some of the available research and findings regarding what I have written, ones that blend with the body of experience I have shared.

First and foremost, my passion toward the validity and utility of the information within these pages rests upon the fact that I have personally seen it, lived it, and benefited from the positive results as a seasoned manager over many years. I know this stuff works independent of my personal views because of my many times teaching the "Burden of Command" course, through my hundreds of lectures to hundreds of students who have *always* provided extremely positive feedback and consistently tell me how the course informed them at their work place because they were able use the information to change their views, increase their effectiveness and promote their self-confidence regarding their command responsibilities, management processes and leadership influence.

However, research and findings matter – they matter a whole bunch – and I feel compelled to review the results and findings from some of the latest studies regarding this important subject. In recent years, there have been many studies involving the concepts involving two types of leaders: the transformational and the transactional.

A transformational leader is one who stimulates interest and attention, inspires, generates awareness, and buys in on organizational goals, develops others to a higher level of ability, and motivates and provides context to consider others interest over one's own. Many researchers note that transformational leadership is made up of four components:

1. Idealized influence

2. Inspirational motivation

3. Intellectual stimulation

4. Individual consideration

On the other hand, the transactional leader is one who rewards or disciplines based upon the subordinate's performance. The transactional leader places emphasis upon direction and task results, work requirements and standards, and subordinate compliance and performance. Transactional leaders believe in rewards and punishments as a means to influence subordinate's conduct, behavior, and performance within the job.

Many studies have found that the transformational leader is more effective, has higher rates of employee satisfaction, and maintains higher levels of group performance. A common theme of behavior observed and integral of a transformational leader's character is their social and emotional intelligence.

John D. Mayer and Peter Salovey's research produced this great quote in 1997 sparking the emotional intelligence fire: "Emotional intelligence involves the ability to perceive accurately, appraise, and express emotion; the ability to access and/or generate feelings when they facilitate thought; the ability to understand emotion and emotional knowledge; and the ability to regulate emotions to promote emotional and intelligent growth."

Enter the writing of Daniel Goleman, that of the vast array of issues and information regarding the notion of emotional intelligence importance. Goleman rocketed the entire science of leadership framework to another level, articulating strategic and tactical means on how to grow and develop oneself and those around him to become aware, astute, and meaningful in the workplace. So many of us were or are promoted to a position of leadership without the benefit of proper training and resources; we are thrown in to either sink or swim. It doesn't have to and shouldn't be that way.

Goleman, and my readings from John Maxwell's great leadership books, forged my intent to design and write the "Burden of Command" course that has led to this book. Rusty Andrews, Fred Stephens, and Debbie Shaw, three training professionals at the GBI, gave me the opportunity and stage to teach it, and Dr. Archie Rainey at Columbus State University's Command College gave me the opportunity to develop it.

I present the below findings that continue to this day, blended in the light of my experience, to provide my closing capstone for the arch of this book. This is principal because of current developments that identify the traits and characteristics of the "contemporary employee," the latest generation of employee combined with their use of new technologies and angles of view that bring a whole new array of issues into the workplace. Today's leader must embrace, adapt, and evolve to incorporate the best skill sets available to promote the best results as a Commander. The research is both interesting and revealing and can create a path of understanding and consideration when used in the correct situational context.

Gennaro F. Vito and George E. Higgins of the University of Louisville in Kentucky found in their 2010 study entitled, "Examining the Validity of the Leadership Challenge Inventory: the Case for Law Enforcement," that the leadership challenge model is valid for understanding leadership capabilities among law enforcement officers and supports the use of the model. A second study by Vito, Suresh, and Richards published in, "Policing - An International Journal of Police Strategies and Management" in 2011, surveyed the opinions of 126 police mangers in 26 states regarding their ideal leadership style given the choices from servant, autocratic, and laissez-faire leadership styles. The study revealed a strong preference for servant leadership, rejecting the autocratic and laissez-fare

A similar study by Dr. Joseph A. Schafer of Southern Illinois University; while serving as a visiting researcher at the FBI behavioral science unit at the FBI National academy, Schafer completed a similar survey that found the following traits of effective leaders:

- Set a proper example and demonstrate trustworthiness.
- Consider input from others.

- Accept responsibility and admit mistakes.
- Make informed decisions based on appropriate research and study.
- Treat all employees fairly and with dignity.
- Allow subordinates to handle duties commensurate with their skills and authority level.

Dr. Schafer highlights the fact that effective leaders may be those who continually strive toward self-improvement and how such ongoing pursuit ensures others will emulate them and strengthen the leadership performance around them.

An infinitely interesting study by Steven A. Murphy and Edward N. Dodge of Carleton University in Ottawa titled "The Four I's of Police Leadership: A Case Study Heuristic," provides additional support for transformational leadership training. This study used a framework of transformational leadership theory that was meaningful in describing conduct within a convenient heuristic comprised of the four I's: Individual consideration; Idealized influence; Inspirational motivation; and Intellectual stimulation. Murphy and Dodge concluded that transformational leaders have particular relational strengths that serve to elevate levels of commitment, work satisfaction and motivation.

Found that transformational leaders have particular relational strengths that serve to elevate levels of commitment, work satisfaction and motivation. In contrast to these studies, Joseph A. Schafer published findings from his FBI academy study using an open-ended survey of mid-career managers to attempt to understand the traits and habits a group of supervisors perceived in leaders they characterized as ineffective. Based upon a consensus approach, his findings found a framework that linked negative leadership traits with individual organizational outcomes. The respondents identified a number of traits and habits that were common among the ineffective leadership they observed. In particular, there were five acts of commission and omission that emerged as recurrent themes in the survey responses:

Commission behaviors:

1.) Focus on self over others

2.) Ego/arrogance

3.) Closed mindedness

4.) Micro-management

5.) Capriciousness

Omission behaviors:

1.) Poor work ethic

2.) Failure to act

3.) Ineffective communication

4.) Lack of interpersonal skills

5.) Lack of integrity

This survey corroborates so much of what many of us already know about our managers and leaders past and present. These studies focus upon the police profession but are important in many, many professions.

Lastly, I want to focus upon occupational stress and how it can adversely impact work place environment and performance. Stress can – and does – drive people to do things they would normally never do and for some, it can be deadly. Study after study has found the primary stressors for police officers are not the external pressures or dangers of the job, but rather the exerted internally from within the organization and administration.

Dr. Jeanne Stinchcomb found that: "Stress occurs when demands are placed upon an individual that exceed that individual's capacity to deal with them, and that stress intensifies when the individual lacks the means to avoid, alter, or control those demands" Further, Dr. Stinchcomb continues that: "The less control employees have over what they are expected to do and the outcome of their efforts, the more likely they are to experience significant stress." And lastly, she states: "In law enforcement organizations, officers are confronted with an unsupportive management system that causes them to experience stress due to a lack of control, and the less control an officer has over a situation, the more stressful it will be."

Jeremy Davey, Patrica Orbst, and Mary Sheehan found that: "Officers cited organizational stressors to be more severe than operational stressors, primary because they cannot control them."

George Kelling and Mary Ann Pate found that: "While there seems to be concern over how the police behave, there is little concern as to how the police feel as a result of their assigned role, and as to how these feelings correlate with behavior and with emotional and physical well-being."

On the whole, many study results indicate that officer's perception of stress, induced by the traditional organization, could be reduced by leaders adapting and implementing employee participative management practices, is far more detrimental than traditionally perceived stressors.

In March 2013, Sarvesh Satija and Waheeda Khan published an article titled, "Emotional Intelligence as a Predictor of Occupational Stress

Among Working Professionals." They looked at occupational stress as a result of one's duty, one's nature, and one's interaction with her work environment. They considered occupational stress associated with the experience of unpleasant, negative emotions such as tension, anxiety, frustration, anger, and depression resulting from aspects from work. They recognized both the physiological and psychological dimensions of stress. They then turned to examine the nomenclature of emotional intelligence and the influence of emotional intelligence upon occupational stress among working professionals. Their study, "Explicitly demonstrated that emotional intelligence was a significant factor influencing occupational stress." They went on to say: "Hiring individuals with higher levels of emotional intelligence is associated with the organizational performance, and increasing the emotional intelligence in working professionals can reduce the occupational stress of the employees and improve their performance."

Again, we see what an important advantage the habitual mindset and daily struggle to build emotional intelligence skills, competency, servant mentality, good interpersonal communication skills, and fair and open management practices is in today's work place. These leadership and management methods are not limited to police, fire, or government employees; these skills work in both the public and private sector and in many diverse jobs.

Commanders must also be empowered, entrusted, and supported; they also must be given responsibility and held accountable within that responsibility. Today's Commander must possess the skill sets and demonstrate the ability to be an excellent leader and manager at the same time; a Commander must be both, not one and the other.

I use the title "Burden of Command" because of the self-discipline required within the difficulty to sustain that willpower at all times in following that unnatural course that defies the human condition and requires so much effort on our part. It is truly a Burden to Command, especially in the context of the 21st century arena of change and uncertainty.

However, there is good news that you can use to incorporate into you daily routine to keep you in sync and ahead of the curve. Here are 10 axioms, or what I believe to be common truths, to help you navigate through your Command responsibilities:

1. **Be value centric:**
   A conscience lives at the center of every being; it determines how they process and understand right from wrong, good from bad. The values we adopt and hold dear forge our beliefs, influence our thoughts, and mold mindsets. They are quick to form and difficult to change, and they will have a profound effect upon our initial evaluation and decision processes.

2. **Demonstrate premier work ethic:**
   There are two types of people: those who run toward work or those that run away from it. Those that constantly take the initiative to seize the moment to enhance their performance and better themselves and their organization are successful. Those who don't, well, are not. Moreover, successful abilities become a model for others to embrace and replicate. Be passionate about your work and foster that same desire around you.

3. **Be servant driven:**
   An inherit belief and overt attitude that drives behavior and conduct, that demonstrates purposeful and loyal devotion toward the organizational goals and mission over self-centered care or ambitions, lies at the center of this axiom. A servant understands how to effectively lead.

4. **Demonstrate purposeful, caring, and people-sensitive behaviors:**
   Talk about and place emphasis on purpose, the positive things the team does to achieve what is good. Articulate in meaningful terms how everyone's contribution is valuable and important

and how the results matter. Live by what you say, a major component in the evaluation and conclusion of whether a leader is a servant driven person who creates and sustains trust and builds positive relationships among others is how others perceive that leader based upon their experience or the opinions of others. When people see you clothe yourself with humility and put them ahead of your own ambitions, it matters. Moreover, when they see you desire to develop and cultivate them, to make them "better" within the organization, they will far exceed your expectations.

5. **Be a collaborative and communicative Commander:**
   Cooperation, coordination, and collaboration build exemplary teams; motivated and competent teams are the future of a great organization. When fueled with and by great communication, the results will be fabulous. Constantly reach out to partner with others, build relationships, and develop reputation within a positive image; cast vision and articulate purpose to others in specific terms with sincerity and enthusiasm.

6. **Be performance and results oriented:**
   Never settle for the status quo; always desire and demand the best. Be the best and produce or exceed the results expected.

7. **Be patient, but persistent:**
   I use the term "qualified patience" because I believe one needs to embrace the notion that things develop over time, thus the self-discipline one can sustain to let those things mature and be of great benefit in the decision making process, timing for best effect or simple reflection is needed to promote more discovery into the process. However, patience can become a hindrance if one uses it to stall or postpone what needs to be done. Oftentimes, seizing the initiative has a tremendous advantage and is successful component toward achieving the

results sought in any given set of circumstances. This situation regarding the decision to wait or move is one of the most difficult and important aspects of command. Such requires the unique combination of competence and confidence tempered by humility and driven by the information available at the time. The key is maintaining a proactive mindset with the anticipation of probable consequence management. Never ever quit; stay dedicated, devoted, focused, and optimistic. Use optimism as an advantage in adverse circumstances and conditions.

8. **Be growth and development focused:**
   You must develop your competencies and grow your expertise and understanding in your craft before you can teach, coach, or mentor others. Work to make others "better" than you.

9. **Be adaptable to change:**
   Embrace change as a challenge you can win. Know that through adversity comes both strength and opportunity; change facilitates innovation.

10. **Be Innovative:**
    Innovation is the prism of advancement; finding a better way makes a better day and brighter future for everyone. Sustain an ongoing quest to innovate and promote, to create a "culture" dedicated toward new ideas, methods, and ways of achieving your organization's goals and objectives.

Last, but not least, I remember a quote from a "salt of the earth" Georgia farmer, Herbert Daniels, who said: "You run past more in life than you ever catch up with." Remember to leave work at work when you do go home. Spend time with your greatest resource, your family and friends. You cannot place a value on the time you devote and spend with them. They will give you love and strength and provide that needed "decompression time" that builds a positive attitude and optimistic outlook. The time I devoted to my friends, family, and church has paid me huge dividends over the years. A great leader has to have his or her affairs in order first, see to your personal life. In closing, I have tried to provide a simple way to understand a complex responsibility. This responsibility is most important because you exercise control and dominion over other people in an unnatural way to accomplish an important purpose; this is the essence of command. People are tremendously important and are the best resources available. They need to feel important, respected, cared for. They also need to be given responsibility and held accountable for their conduct, performance, and behavior. It is an absolute Burden to Command; it never lets up; it never becomes automatic or natural; it demands dedication, devotion, and constant work every day of your life. My most reoccurring prayer is, "God, please protect me from myself." You will never get it right all the time, but if you strive toward being the best Commander you can be, and strive to follow the course outlined within these pages, you will do well.

THANK YOU

To my very special friends and mentors, Dr. Archie Rainey and Dr. Curtis McClung who inspired me through their love of those in our profession to continue to strive to be the best possible at any age because life is about purpose more than anything else. The heart, soul, and sweat they put into the Command College has touched many lives and produced many fabulous executives to lead Georgia Law Enforcement. Archie gave me the opportunity of a lifetime to play a small role in their historic and meaningful endeavor.

To Debbie Shaw, Rusty Andrews, Fred Stephens, and Tom Davis who were the catalyst for my dedication to research and development of the materials for the Burden of Command course creation.

To the many agents I had the privilege and honor to supervise over the years, who made me look good, to Eliza Noles, who encouraged me to begin this book, and the many students from my many Burden of Command classes that gave me the motivation to sustain the work to complete this book, to Skip Latson, the Training Director at Atlanta/Carolina's HITDA that kept me inspired during the process from class evaluations and positive feedback.

To Jonathan Moore, my editor who does all that he can to make me presentable in print.

To my longtime friends and mentors, Tate Brown, Johnny McGlamery, Dupont K. Cheney, Romie Waters and those that continue their counsel to me today, Roy Harris, Harry Coursey, Bob Ingram, Dale Mann, Charles Sikes, and Bill Hitchens.

My late parents, my father, Jack who taught me values, and my mother, Carolyn who taught me how to be a gentleman, both nurtured and molded me in preparation for life, and my siblings Jack, Joe and Lynn and their families who are a true blessing from above.

A very special thanks to God who supports me and provides for my works, my love for people, the ideas and wisdom to record on paper and gives me the three most important people in my life, who I have tried my very best to be the best for them because they have been for me. My wife, soul mate and best friend Anita, my eldest son J.B, advisor, assistant and master of many things and my courageous, lion heart and passionate youngest son Mac. Without these three I could not exist.

To the reader, Godspeed in your endeavors to lead,

"It's a burden to command, but a blessing to have the opportunity."

John B. Edwards,
January, 2014

CASE STUDIES FOR THOUGHT
AND DISCUSSION

Case Study I involves a newly appointed police captain that demonstrates problematic management traits that cause a perfect storm of work place complaints, while Case Study II uses an example of a restaurant manager whom demonstrates "proven leadership characteristics" that result in increased revenues, more cost efficient operations and more effective service. Use these two scenarios for comparison and contrast to evaluate the leadership traits and management strategies used in each scenario.

CASE STUDY I

A lieutenant is promoted to the captain of a work unit. The work unit consists of an existing lieutenant, two sergeants, and sixteen officers.

Upon arrival to the work unit, the new captain assesses the administrative and operational inner workings of the office. He is notified that his office has just received two new laptop computers. He immediately assigns himself one of the new ones and then transfers his old computer to one of the junior officers in the work unit. The second new computer, he gives to the most senior officer in the work unit.

He looks through files and conducts several file reviews. He notices that there are many closed case reports that have final dispositions that do not reach his expectation in the degree of specificity or manner that they are written. He immediately constructs a memo for the officers to reopen these cases and correct these dispositions then re-close.

The captain does not seek or request input from any other officers to include the lieutenant or the two sergeants, he pushes everyone ahead with his own agenda and his my way or the highway mentality. When one of the sergeants identifies a potential issue afoot in the work place the captain dresses him down in front of other officers and lets him know that he is the captain and already knew about the issue.

The captain changes shifts without consulting anyone and crafts and submits the units next year's budget (normally the lieutenant's job) without consulting with the lieutenant or anyone else within the work place.

The call roster in this office is unique due to the fact that it separates call for officers by days and then has separate weekend calls. The new captain learned that this has been the case at this work unit for many years. Although this may be the custom of this office, it would be much easier upon the supervisors with all of the duties that they incur to change the call roster where a particular officer is on call for that entire particular week. He moves forward and changes the way the call roster is completed.

While checking administrative reports, the captain determines that car reports are very difficult to check behind due to the fact that the officers are not rounding off their gas purchases when pumping gas. He immediately put out a memo to all officers to pump their gas to even figures on the pumps. Such will save time and energy while reviewing car reports monthly.

An advantage this captain has in this promotion in this work unit is that one officer in the office is a career long friend and confidant. He has had a relationship with this officer for many years and fully trusts him. He finds himself using this officer as an information source regarding the work unit's activities, conduct, and behavior. He also confides in this officer in some issues that he doesn't even discuss with his lieutenant. He has found this officer to be a valuable resource within the work unit and feels free to tell him anything at any time no matter how sensitive.

As the new captain continues through the months ahead to bring the work unit into the "ship shape" status he desires, he regularly talks about his ambition to be promoted to major one day and that the work unit team must mirror the successful processes he has enhanced.

During a very busy time for the work unit, the captain conducts a file review. The file review is conducted out of the presence of the principle officer who investigated the case or any of their supervisors. The captain closes several cases administratively on his own due to the fact the files lack updates and his opinion is the cases can go no further. Such is in his mission to have a very efficient and effective administration.

The lieutenant comes to the captain and advises that deputy chief Joe Jones called regarding an old homicide case from the 80's and new leads developed. The lieutenant told the captain that deputy chief Jones wanted to know what steps the unit had taken since his call to the captain several weeks ago. The lieutenant told the deputy chief he didn't know anything about the issue and would talk to the captain and call deputy chief Jones back.

The captain has set up pristine filing systems over the last several months. One of the things that he is most proud of is his file on every officer where he keeps emails where he directs them to do things. Such is a way he can keep up with the directions he gives and ensures they are followed. This culture he has developed of talking to officers only by email documents the agents work performance.

An officer comes in the captain's office regarding a homicide case he has worked where he received two signed admissions from two co-defendants. The officer feels good about his case until he is cautioned by a District Attorney on the problems that may occur with the "Bruton Rule." (A point of law that requires the right of confrontation of adversarial witnesses) The captain advises the officer that "it is a good case, don't worry about it", and he will get with them later. During the same period of time, another officer pressures the captain on a case regarding a lead that was sent to a fellow officer to cover for him. This officer cannot successfully prepare his case for the District Attorney until the other officer completes the lead. The other officer in question has told the captain that the lead is not important and it deals with an issue in the case that has nothing to do with the prosecution and is "just a rumor" that doesn't need to be followed up. He tells that officer to table the case and they will move forward later.

The Captain decides the units community relations program does not involved him enough, he contacts the neighborhood and business representatives and tells them that he will be coming to the weekly meetings and has established a new program of his own that he will implement. The Captain does not consult with his Lieutenant or the Sargent that is responsible for the management of the program who has run the weekly meetings for over three years.

The on-call officer for the upcoming week has just been notified of a mandatory training day during their call. The officer reports this conflict that is beyond her control to the captain. The captain tells her "find someone to swap call with you, and then let me know."

After a quarterly car inspection, the captain finds one officer out of the 16 that has not been changing his oil in a timely fashion. He will not tolerate this due to the problem with keeping good vehicles within the work unit. He calls an immediate office meeting and gets onto everyone about the importance of oil changes and how they should ensure they maintain their vehicles.

The chief drives down to visit as a result of a successful conclusion to a major incident the office worked. The chief praises everyone regarding the outstanding work performance and end results. The captain replies, "Me and my officers worked hard. I put a lot into this case."

The captain calls an important office meeting regarding an upcoming inspection of the office. On the day before the meeting, an officer calls the captain very sympathetically and tells him that his wife (a school teacher) cannot get off of work to carry their daughter to the orthodontist regarding an infection that has occurred with her braces. The officer goes on to advise that the grandparents are out of town and not available to help and he must be the one responsible for carrying the daughter to the doctor. The captain becomes angry and tells him that he will work with him this time, but in the future he needs to have alternative choices regarding child care.

At the office meeting after the captain covers his directives for inspection, he talks about the upcoming holidays and an office Christmas party. The captain tells everyone in the work unit that he wants to have a dinner at a local restaurant he likes, it will be Dutch treat for everyone involved, and that everyone will bring a present not to be over $40 for playing "Bad Santa" after the meal.

The Christmas party occurs. The lieutenant, one sergeant and three officers are the only staffs that show up. The captain learns from his trusted officer that he has the relationship with that there are mass rumors throughout the office that the inspection team responsible for the office inspection has received numerous complaints regarding the stress in the unit and the captains leadership and management skills.

His blind ambition, self-centered mind set and authoritative and micro-management styles were a recipe for disaster.

CASE STUDY II

A new manager has just been hired for Joe's House of Fine Food, a restaurant in an up and coming community. The restaurant has a senior executive chef who has been running the kitchen for 5 years, 2 sous-chefs and 6 cooks with 2 dish washers and 2 bus boys who take care of the cleaning of tables, 6 waiters or waitresses, 2 maître d's and 2 bartenders make up the other staff.

The restaurant opens five nights a week, from 5pm to 9pm Tuesday through Saturday. The staff arrives at 3 pm each working day to prepare and ready the restaurant. There has been a history of tardiness, poor attitude and argument among employees. Revenues are down and morale is low. There are no in-house policies or procedures in existence. The executive chef is upset over the new hiring of the manager because he wanted the job and thought the younger less experienced manager would be a mistake for the restaurant. The restaurant has come under scrutiny from a poor health department rating in the kitchen, poor service from the servers and bartenders drinking while working. Patrons have posted to the restaurants face book page that the bathrooms were "nasty" and the food quality is "poor." One posting noted being served an "unclean tea glass with lip stick on the rim."

The new manager has been told by the owners to shape up the business and replace people if needed. The restaurant specializes in seafood and the menu has steak as the only alternative. The manager conducts research, studying the different aspects of seafood procurement, preparation and service. She looks to other professionals in her field regarding the pro's and con's regarding a restaurant with such a narrow specialty. She searches the internet for comments and postings under the restaurant's name

The manager then plans individual meetings where she can learn about the employees and they can learn about her. She knows this will be an opportunity to connect, communicate and learn. She intends to listen, learn and evaluate.

On the managers first day, she meets with the executive chef and makes inquiry and probes into the executive chef's opinions, beliefs and theories regarding the Restaurant's administration and operation. She aggressively listens and takes notes. The manager assures the chef that his interview has been meaningful and she will follow up with the chef later as she assesses the functions and systems in the restaurant.

The executive chef has several very good ideas, but some are not. The manger implements a couple of the executive chef's ideas and credits him for their innovation and value. Then the manager turns to a problem identified regarding the executive chef because there are several menu items the executive chef will not terminate that simply do not sell. The manager obtains the specific sales, inventory and cost information provides to the executive chef for him to evaluate the results of the data. She outlines the perimeters of the decision criterion, and then delegates to him the opportunity to provide an alternative or solution. She knows that if the chef cannot change and come up with a solution she will make the changes and incorporate them into the operation, but she wants his "buy in" and "ownership" in the process.

The manager then meets with the souse chefs separately, the cooks, washers and bus boys. From these meetings the manager identifies specific problems, chronic complaints and is able to shape a picture of the totality of kitchen operations. An example is found with the two dishwashers who have never been trained on the operation of an automatic dish washer purchased a year ago. Once they were trained and used the equipment properly all the plates and glasses were immaculately cleaned. The souse chefs have a problem with the way the executive chef requires them to manage the fryer, after they are given the specific reasons behind the executive chef's concerns and explained the consequences attached to a failure to comply, they approved and appreciated their duty toward that requirement.

Next the manager interviewed each staff member, the waiters and waitresses, bartenders and maître d's carefully listening and noting consistencies and inconsistencies regarding job duties, roles and responsibilities. One of the bar tenders had developed her distinct method and manner of handling wine service at the bar that was totally different from the way the corporation accomplished the task from where the manager received her training. The bar tenders methods met health standards, were safe, did not waste product or cause an additional cost, thus the manager let the bar tender continue with her custom.

Additionally, from these interviews the manager learned about old methods that new technology outdated. This resulted in a change of customs that made the work easier, more staff efficient and cost effective. Moreover, the manager received a relational and organizational view through the lens of the staff to compare with his education, experience and vision and expectations of the owners. Her motto to the staff was "let's work smarter."

The manager then inspected, analyzed, evaluated and compared the computerized business records, sales, and inventories to the information from the interviews she conducted. She correlated data and information to obtain a complete and global view of the business. The manager then examines each position and designs a job description specific to that position. The job descriptions rely heavily upon the information gleaned from the employee interviews. The manager meets with each employee goes over the job description obtains buy in from the employees and ensures they understand the expectations placed upon them. The manger then created policy from the ground up that everyone knew, understood, and had input into its design features. The manager provided the job descriptions and the policies to the owners to sign off on and to adopt as their policies.

The manager trained every employee on the policies and ensured they understood them. These policies covered everything from service to cleaning of bathrooms to prohibition of any employee drinking while working. She places emphasis upon the zero-tolerance violations and the adverse consequences involved.

She cast the vision of the owners, the restaurants purpose, goals and objectives. She demonstrates positive attitudes and sincere optimism toward the restaurants future.

The manager then scheduled a meeting with the executive chef and sous-chefs to look at other ideas regarding the menu and making dishes from seasonal and fresh ingredients that can be purchased locally at a reduced price.

The manager uses this opportunity to highlight each chef's idea and empathized with the executive chef's views when and where he could. The manager was constantly soliciting ideas from her staff regarding how they could serve patrons better and produce premier products. The manager worked hard and joins in when and where she can to help in service, the kitchen and cleaning tables, always conscience and loyal to her priorities in her management responsibility. The manager periodically checks the bathroom, examines glassware, visits the bar, thanks and solicits feedback from patrons and taste the food regularly. The manager uses her relationship with patrons to promote positive social media communications.

The manager constantly observes and stays engaged with the restaurants staff in the oversight of their administrative and operational responsibilities. She encourages, praises, mentors, coaches and corrects. She delegates, gives ownership and lets them work. She holds herself and everyone else accountable to the job requirements while constantly creating a positive and productive environment.

Revenues climb, tips soar and operations improve, the manager credits the restaurant staff in front of the owners with the employees watching and listening and highlights their efforts to better the business. She gives them credit and exposer for their input and work.

One of the waiters approaches the manager and tells her that he is very fond of her and respects her. He asks if she would go out with him on a date on Sunday night. The manager responds that she is flattered and honored that he asked but it would be improper for her to have a personal relationship with a member of the staff.

One waiter has been late on two occasions, on both occasions the waiter says his mother is sick and prevented him for leaving on time. The manger demonstrates empathy regarding the mother, but outlines to the waiter of his importance and value toward the success of the restaurant and how being on time is so important. The manager asked what she can do to help the waiter. They come up with a plan together regarding doing things earlier for his mother and develop a plan. The waiter is on time from that point on.

A bus boy develops a pattern of being late, after three meetings with follow up meetings from the manager and no change in the employee's conduct, the manager ensures the bus boy knows the rules, has had a time to explain his conduct and has been given an opportunity to participate in the planning to change his behavior to meet the job requirements. After these efforts to mentor and coach fail, the owners and their legal advisors are consulted and the bus boy is terminated.

One of the bar tenders is caught drinking, in direct violation of the policy. The policy calls for termination for violation. The manager calls upon the owners, their lawyer and the decision is made to terminate the bar tender.

The manager makes it a priority to encourage and praise the staff when they do good work. She also looks for ways to include them in decision making, innovations, ideas and opportunities. She forges the notion they are all owners in the restaurant and as the restaurant grows and prospers so will they. The manager constantly solicits feedback from staff, she maintains a professional culture and stays engaged. She is careful to not high jack or take anyone's job responsibilities, but is quick to lend a helping hand to everyone. She also provides clear unambiguous expectations, relays upon a foundation of sound policy and good procedure that everyone knows and understands. She mentors and coaches' individuals when their performance or behavior does not meet job expectations or standards. She does everything to remain involved and engaged, but if they do not perform she does not walk past them or work around them, she deals with them.

Her purpose driven, analytic gathering, service motivated and results orientated mentality in combination with her use of people skills and leadership style she demonstrates are a driver for success.

RECOMMENDED READING LIST

Primal Leadership
by Daniel Goleman, Richard Boyatzis, Annie McKee
Publisher: Harvard Business Review Press (2004)
ISBN-10: 1422168034
ISBN-13: 978-1422168035

The One Minute Manager
by Kenneth H. Blanchard, Spencer Johnson
Publisher: William Morrow (2003)
ISBN-10: 0688014291
ISBN-13: 978-0688014292

The 21 Irrefutable Laws of Leadership:
Follow Them and People Will Follow You.
by John C. Maxwell
Publisher: Thomas Nelson (2013)
ISBN-10: 0785288376
ISBN-13: 978-0785288374

The 360 Degree Leader:
Developing Your Influence from Anywhere in the Organization
by John C. Maxwell
Publisher: Thomas Nelson (2001)
ISBN-10: 0785260927
ISBN-13: 978-0785260929

Developing the Leader Within You
by John C. Maxwell
Publisher: Thomas Nelson (2005)
ISBN-10: 0785281126
ISBN-13: 978-0785281122

The Situational Leader
by Dr. Paul Hersey
Publisher: Warner Books (1985)
ISBN-10: 0446513423
ISBN-13: 978-0446513425

Leadership and the One Minute Manager:
Increasing Effectiveness Through Situational Leadership
by Ken Blanchard , Patricia Zigarmi, Drea Zigarmi
Publisher: William Morrow (1999)
ISBN-10: 0688039693
ISBN-13: 978-0688039691

Management
by Peter F. Drucker
Publisher: Harper Business (2008)
ISBN-10: 0061252662
ISBN-13: 978-0061252662

It's Your Ship: Management Techniques from the Best Damn Ship in the Navy
by D. Michael Abrashoff
Publisher: Business Plus (2012)
ISBN-10: 145552302X

BIBLIOGRAPHY

Abrashoff, D. Michael. It's your ship management techniques from the best damn ship in the Navy. Concordville, Pa.: Soundview Executive Book Summaries ;, 2007.

Andreescu, Viviana and Gennaro F. Vito. "An exploratory study on ideal leadership behaviour: the opinions of American police managers." International Journal of Police Science & Management In-Press. 12, no. 4 (2010): 567-583.

Batts, Anthony, Sean Michael Smoot, and Ellen Scrivner. "Police Leadership Challenges in a Changing World. " National Institute of Justice. (2012): 1-24

Blanchard, Kenneth H., and Spencer Johnson. The one minute manager. New York: Morrow, 1982.

Davey, Jeremy, Patrica Obst, and Mary Sheehan. "Work demographics and officers' perceptions of the work environment which add to the prediction of at risk alcohol consumption within an Australian police sample." Policing: An International Journal of Police Strategies & Management, 23 no. 1 (2000): 69-81

Douglass, Earl Leroy. The Snowden-Douglass Sunday school lessons, 1946: practical expositions of the international sunday school lessons. New York: Macmillan, 1945.

Blanchard, Kenneth H., Patricia Zigarmi, and Drea Zigarmi. Leadership and the one minute manager: increasing effectiveness through situational leadership. New York: Morrow, 1985.

Drucker, Peter F., and Joseph A. Maciariello. Management. Rev. ed. New York, NY: Collins, 2008.

Edwards, John B. "The Major Incident Quadrahydral. "FBI Law Enforcement Bulletin 78, no 8 (2009): 21

Frankfurt, Harry G.. On bullshit. Princeton, NJ: Princeton University Press, 2005.

Goleman, Daniel, Richard E. Boyatzis, and Annie McKee. Primal leadership: realizing the power of emotional intelligence. Boston, Mass.: Harvard Business School Press, 2002.

Goleman, Daniel, and Richard Boyatzis. "Social Intelligence and the Biology of Leadership." Harvard Business Review, September 2008.

Harrison, Jeffrey S. and R. Edward Freeman. "Stakeholders, social responsibility, and performance: empirical evidence and theoretical perspectives." Academy of management Journal 42, no. 5 (1999): 479-485.

Hersey, Paul. The situational leader. New York, NY: Warner Books, 19851984.

Kelling, George and Mary Ann Pate. "The Person-Role fit in Policing: The Current Knowledge and Future Research." Job Stress and the Police Officer (1975): 117-129.

Maxwell, John C.. The 21 irrefutable laws of leadership: follow them and people will follow you. Nashville, Tenn.: Thomas Nelson Publishers, 1998.

Maxwell, John C.. The 360-degree leader: developing your influence from anywhere in the organization. Nashville: Nelson Business, 2005.

Maxwell, John C., and John C. Maxwell. Developing the leader within you Developing the leaders around you. Nashville, Tenn.: Thomas Nelson, 2009.

Murphy, Steven A. and Edward N. Drodge. "Four I's of Police Leadership: A Case Study Heuristic." International Journal of Police Science and Management 6, no. 1 (2004): 1-15

Pollock, Joycelyn M.. Ethical dilemmas and decisions in criminal justice. 5th ed. Belmont, CA: Thomson/Wadsworth, 2007.

Salovey and John D. Mayer, Peter. "Emotional Intelligence." Imagination, Cognition and Personality 9, no. 3 (1990): 1-1.

Satija, Sarvesh and Waheeda Khan. "Emotional Intelligence as a Predictor of Occupational Stress Among Working Professionals. " Aweshkar Research Journal 15, no. 1 (2013): 79

Schafer, Joseph A.. Effective leadership in policing: successful traits and habits. Durham, N.C.: Carolina Academic Press, 2013.

Stinchcomb, Jeanne B.. "Searching For Stress In All The Wrong Places: Combating Chronic Organizational Stressors In Policing." Police Practice and Research 5, no. 3 (2004): 259-277.

Vera, Dusya and Mary Crossan. "Organizational Learning, Knowledge Management, and Intellectual Capital: An Integrative Conceptual Model. " The Handbook of Organizational Learning & Knowledge Management (2000): 1-26.

Vito, Gennaro F., and George E. Higgins. "Examining the Validity of The Leadership Challenge Inventory: The Case for Law Enforcement." International Journal of Police Science & Management 12, no. 3 (2010): 305-319.

Vito, Gennaro F., Geetha Suresh, and George E. Richards. "Emphasizing the Servant in Public Service: The Opinions of Police Managers. "Policing – An International Journal of Police Strategies and Management 34, no. 4 (2011): 674-686.

Willis, James J. . "Improving Police: What's Craft Got to do With It?. " Police Foundation 16. (2013): 1-14.

Made in the USA
Charleston, SC
18 July 2014